Short Tall Stories

Short Tall Stories

Stanley J. White

Beyond the Third Dimension Press

To Heather and Frank

Copyright © 2022 by Stanley J. White

All Rights Reserved.

No part of this book may be used or reproduced by any means, graphic, electronic, or mechanical, including photocopying, recording, taping, or by any information storage retrieval system without the written permission of the publisher except in the case of brief quotations embodied in critical articles and reviews.

ISBN 978-0-9689463-3-6

Cover and title pages photo by Stan J. White

www.stanjwhite.com

Contents

Acknowledgements vii	Little Black Book 123
Foreword. ix	Camera Obscura. 127
A Perfect Murder 11	Lifelike. 149
Gossamer Strings. 15	The Green Eye of the Little Yellow God 151
Asylum 27	
Kafka's Great-Great-Great-Grandson 35	A Cock and Bull Story 157
Rufus and Ridley 39	Duel in iPod Time 161
Affairs of a Welsh Town 49	Virtual Virtuosity 165
	All That Glitters 167
Myth of Myths 53	Early Wheat 169
Carnations and Reincarnations. 63	Father's 2x4 by 8 Foot Cedar Stud 185
Moon Song without Words 69	A Visit with My Grandfather 189
Robinson Crusoe 77	What Heaven is Like . . . 197
The Banjo 85	The Photographer's Song. 201
A Black Pebble 89	
The Bottom Step 93	Love in a Teacup 205
The Library Card 103	Congratulations on your finding a bottle with a genie. 215
The Small Space beneath the Ceiling 109	
One Late Payment 113	Like a Child's Balloon 219
The Dog, Parish 117	

Acknowledgements

This will be my last book. I am deeply grateful to my dear friend Bernadette Rule who did most of the hands-on preparation, without which, this book could never have been published. Thanks also go to April Bulmer who assisted with the editing, and to my IT son-in-law, Frank, for the technical assistance, and also to my publisher, Greg Smith of blindpigpress, and a special thank you to Richard Van Holst.

Thanks also go to my many writer friends, who by association over the years, maintained my interest.

Books (poetry) previously published by the author: *Four Solitudes, About Time, Beyond the Third Dimension,* and *Ars Poetica and Other Poems.*

Chapbooks: *Itinerant, Poems One, Annum, Anomalies of Violence,* and *Oddities.*

The following books and chapbooks were written in various collaborations with other poets: *Quaere, Portals, Telling Lies, Double Take, Seven by Seven, A Week of Thoughts* and *Banshee Songs.*

Thanks also to the following: *The Cambridge Writers Collective,* and *The Brantford Poetry Workshop.*

Ars Poetica and Other Poems by Stanley J. White 2022, selections from 40 years of writing, is also available on paperback or ebook from lulu.com.

Foreword

These stories have been written over the last 40 years. As each idea came to me, I built a short story around it. When I was a boy, I was intrigued by stories of various kinds: adventure tales, humorous stories, love stories, science fiction and tales of the absurd. Especially memorable were: Jules Verne's *Journey to the Centre of the Earth*; the horror of *The Pit and the Pendulum* by Edgar Allan Poe, and that of *The Monkey's Paw* by W.W. Jacobs; and the humour of Jerome K. Jerome's *Three Men in a Boat*.

    The short story, with its brevity, seems to me to be an ideal package for our urgent world. I wrote these stories in memory of the boy who read the great authors. They are tales of adventure, humour, love, science fiction, and the absurd.

A Perfect Murder

That he was a senior, whose criminal past concealed only an occasional ticket for speeding, and that he had led close to a blameless life and was highly respected in his church circle, gave his need even more urgency. For no apparent reason, and out of the blue, he found in late middle-age he was possessed with the urge to kill somebody. Perhaps it was because after his wife died he lived alone, and life was mind-bogglingly monotonous

He had watched TV programs in which killers, thinking they had "got away with it" found they had been tripped up by some unlikely event, some quirk of coincidence, somebody somewhere had noticed a car number plate, or some facet of forensic science had been overlooked. It was a challenge, but notwithstanding, he felt confident that with care he could commit the perfect murder. Clearly, he would have to avoid making even one tiny error that could put the police onto his track. The trick was not to leave anything to coincidence.

He would avoid firearms—they were noisy and too easily traced. A fluke gave him an opportunity for an alternative. On one of his drives, he stopped for lunch in a small town where there was an outdoor flea market... a few tables, and some vendors selling out of the trunks of their cars. One seller had a small modern crossbow, the kind used for hunting that fired a short, metal arrow called a bolt. It was exactly the tool for the job. It was a cash sale and there were no indoor store cameras there to record him.

Cars also were too easily traced, so he decided to use a bicycle for transport. There would be no obvious motive for his killing since he would choose a complete stranger. He would call him "the Dark Stranger".

On the evening of a fine day, he drove to a nearby town, leaving his car parked on the main street's free parking zone, and took off into the countryside on his bicycle. He eventually came across a man walking along one of the smaller side roads. This man, he decided, would be "the Dark Stranger". Cycling past him, he rounded a bend until he was out of sight. Taking the bike with him over a gate and finding a gap in the hedge, with crossbow loaded, he waited for his victim. There were no dwellings in the area from which he might be observed and the road was empty in both directions. It proved an easy aim with his laser sight. At some twenty or so feet, the silent bolt found its mark. Conveniently, the man fell into the ditch at the side of the road. His body might not be discovered for days. Having achieved his objective without problems, he cycled back to his car. He then drove back to his home town where he stopped at a local pub, got stinking drunk, gave his car keys to the barman and took a taxi home. If necessary, he was sure the barman and the cab driver would remember him.

He had been wearing gloves throughout, and he spent the next several days shredding the clothes he had worn, including the shoes. He disassembled the crossbow and the bicycle so that everything was in tiny fragments, which he deposited in rivers, ponds, garbage bins miles from his home town, until everything to do with the murder had been distributed in a thousand places. He even resisted the temptation to follow the subsequent events, police announcements etc. as they pertained to the crime, feeling it might look suspicious if he took unusual interest. He was convinced he had committed the perfect crime.

* * *

Several weeks passed before the bombshell... he learned his son had been charged with murder. He was floored to find the man his son was charged with murdering was his "Dark Stranger". It ultimately turned out that the two men had an association, and that there was great rancor between them. In fact, they had recently fought, and the police were brought in. On the night of the murder, they were scheduled to meet each other. If that wasn't enough to arouse suspicion, his son also belonged to a local hunting club in which they sometimes used crossbows. The police figured his motive was that the man had been playing around with his wife.

To save his son he confessed, but the police didn't believe him. Show us some proof, they said, but of course he couldn't, since all was beyond recovery. So thorough had he been that even he couldn't produce a shred of evidence that he had committed the crime. It was obviously a case of a father trying to take the blame for his son's sins.

The evidence against his son was purely circumstantial but it was so prolific and damaging that it took the jury just four hours to find him guilty.

He was sentenced to 25 to life.

Gossamer Strings

"Akil! Akil!" I shouted, but he didn't hear me. It's well over fifty years since I had seen him but I would recognise that gait anywhere.

He was at the Albion football grounds, but by the time I had made my way down from the stands he was well clear of the D4 exit ramp and had disappeared in the dispersal of the crowd.

Considering our humble beginnings, the world has been good to me, and I wondered how he had fared. Besides, I still owed him money—his share of the pot—a large sum in those days but now barely enough to buy a carton of cigarettes. In the main, I was curious to know how the story ended.

Back then, I did not think too much about it. But some things acquire a greater significance as time passes, as though time gives gravity to understanding. It never occurred to me that there was also a rationale to madness. Now experience has made me a little less arbitrary.

In those days, to be born English was to feel superior to every other race; it was in the genes. But the English, perhaps realising that such arrogance if turned upon itself could be destructive, arranged their social order in levels of inferiority, down from a stuttering though socially omnipotent king.

As kids from lower working class families we were on the bottom rung, but Akil, with his club foot and his evident Romany blood, did not even make the scale. I always thought of him as being younger than the rest of the gang. In fact, he was just smaller. The blunt truth was that he was a runt.

His real name was Mavety, Carlos Mavety.

His mother was a large, gloomy Irish woman who worked as a cleaner in a local foundry. She had Carlos late in life and it was clear that he had gypsy blood in him. That would make another story.

They lived, the two of them, in a cheap flat over a butcher's shop on Belcher Street.

When I speak of a gang, I mean something quite different from what is meant by the term today. We were just a group of kids. I suppose the purpose of our association was to conjure a world in which we could establish our own values. Our activities were a series of dares, and there was not one of the stunted trees that had not been climbed by every one of us. We knew each derelict factory intimately and had climbed its crumbling bricks, negotiated its broken windows and clambered precariously over its rusting beams. If vandalism accrued from our activities it was the innocent by-product of the process of proving ourselves.

The Black Country from which we hailed was aptly named. Seeded with heavy industry and nurtured for a hundred and fifty years by a coterie of self-made men, it was now the tailings of the industrial revolution, which after a short hiatus would continue its disintegration in the wake of the imminent war.

Amidst a proliferation of factories, rolling and stamping mills, smelters, a myriad of small casting shops, two large iron works, the coal mines and all the die, tool and machinery manufactories needed to sustain them, stood a priapism of stacks spewing the residues of soft coal. The ravages of utility lay ugly across the environment.

At night, a threshold of ferric rumble, like an imminent metal storm, was lighted by the blast of distant Bessemer.

Smutty houses in bedraggled towns stunted the miles of slag in a black landscape dalmatian'd in winter by the snows, infiltrated in the spring by nervous grasses. In a dry summer, the lifeless cinders dominated, as though a night sky had fallen.

But for us, impatient upon the threshold of youth where all of the world is mystery, there was nothing satanic about it. It was home, and we were held wonder-struck in this riotous calamity of electricity, magnetism and Nineteenth Century mechanics gone mad.

The gang's headquarters was the pithead of the abandoned Peerless mine. We had forced a rotting door. It was a dank, cheerless place, dirty and full of rusting machinery, but it gave us privacy. I shall never forget the plink, plink clarity of the sound of water drips as they fell into the echo chamber of the mine shaft, nor the salty choke of the coal dust as it caught in the throat like the dry powder of an inorganic curry. The shaft had been boarded up thirty years ago but we had pried loose some of the planks. A rusty bolt dropped into the mine took an eternity before we heard the hollow plunk as it hit water.

There is a kind of cussedness about kids at times, as though the devil gets into them. I've forgotten now how it started, but somehow it got to be a contest as to who would be the first to jump the mine shaft. Usually, after the initial blustering, these discussions were allowed to fizzle out in the interests of self-preservation. This time the potential of the dare gathered a measure of probability and one or two of us began to take the possibility seriously. Then somebody, I don't remember who, dared Carlos. Without warning, in his awkward running shuffle, he launched himself across the cavity, left by the removal of the boards, clearing the gap comfortably. But the rotten wood on the far side collapsed under him and he went straight through.

We stood for seconds, lifeless as characters in a film that had jammed in the gate of the projector. The sound of falling debris, as it hit the water at the bottom of the shaft, broke the spell.

"Yo' orlright mate?" said Colly, our leader, not expecting a reply.

From six feet beneath us, the words—calm, unhurried, and riddled with reverberation—cut to the quick of our anxiety. "I'm 'angin' from a pipe!"

We scurried around. Somebody found an old chain and a wooden beam, and we manoeuvred him out of the shaft, bruised but showing no real distress, while most of us were in a state of shock.

That wasn't the first time that Carlos had shown recklessness, but it would be the last time that any of us dared him to do anything. We could do without the consequences on our consciences.

After that, we nick-named him Achilles, Akil for short.

I never did understand him, for he talked little and there was a matter-of-factness about him that was difficult to penetrate. He had earned our respect for his courage, but in hindsight, except on one occasion, I am not sure that it was courage. Perhaps I am a cynic, but I have never felt comfortable with any word that suggests sacrifice. In the profound complexity of choice, however difficult, don't we all take the easiest path?

Carlos reminded me of the youths that we would see in the newsreels, carrying a crucifix in Catholic ceremonies through the streets of South American cities. I came to understand that he was born to believe. His existence was as grey as the slag around him, and his life offered him so little hope that in the absence of any contact with or knowledge of an institutional religion, he made a faith out of the vacuum.

After the gang broke up we lost touch for a while. Most of us were busy pursuing that other mystery that God had unexpectedly dangled between our legs. Later, Akil worked for *Evesham's Garage & Petrol Pump*. When his mother died, Old Man Evesham let him live in the shed at the back of the shop. It was a primitive place and his only sanitation was an outhouse and the oily sink with the cold tap, against the wall in the larger shed that served as the service bay. It is not surprising that he was not too clean, but all I remember were his shoes with their thick crepe soles. The crepe had spread outward around the shoe uppers from its continuous soaking in oil. He looked as though he were standing on two giant jellyfish.

Akil took no interest in girls. His one consuming passion was his motorbike, an old Triumph that he had bought for a song. He rode it like a maniac amongst the slag tips. One of his favourite stunts was to drive the bike off an old loading ramp. He would compete against himself, gradually increasing the distance that he could keep the bike airborne.

Whippet racing was the sport in those parts. It was illegal, or at least the gambling was, and so to stage the races each Sunday morning, a different site would be chosen in amongst the slag heaps. And so it was common to see twenty or thirty old men in their union shirts, scrawny as cockerel's feet, racing their trained dogs to which they gave more care and attention than their wives. They spoke in a vernacular of servitude, in sing-song voices, each phrase ending on a rising cadence which masked any hint of intellect, giving even profundity an air of the comical. It was not long before they were betting on Akil.

He did not mind; he would have done his stunts anyway. He never did them for acclamation; he was just as happy to do them without an audience and he certainly did not do them for money. But this is where I came in. I felt he should get something out of it, and so I made a deal with him to be his manager for a percentage. Those were difficult times, and for a couple of years we lived on the edge of chapel morality.

We did well from the beginning and it wasn't long before we upstaged the whippets. Folks started to come in from Dudley, Walsall, and from as far as Wolverhampton. We had a few narrow squeaks with the local police constable, but the look-outs would warn us in good time and the crowd would drift away into the surrounding contours of the tips. By the time the constable arrived on his bicycle, there would be nothing but the distant roar of the motorbike as Akil did a quick bunk with me on the pillion.

At first they would bet on the distance that he would jump, but then we started to stack old mine trolleys across the space between the ramps to make the event more of a spectacle. The bookies would pay us a percentage of the lay, and we soon had enough money to build better ramps and to buy Akil an old, though more powerful, Norton to replace the even older Triumph.

Of course, there were times when he came a purler, and he was usually covered in grazes and bruises, but the worst that happened to him was a broken wrist and a few cracked ribs that didn't even slow him down. I never saw him show the least emotion. He appeared utterly fearless.

I had big ideas for us both, and after a year or so, began to explore other possibilities that might make us a few quid. Twice a year there was a fair set up on a corner of the old Billingsley tip. The knocked-down ferris wheels, roundabouts, and stalls would arrive in a procession of trailer caravans on a Monday. By Tuesday the stalls, the coconut shies, the wheel, the over-the-sticks, the whips, the bumper cars, the cakewalk, the helter-skelter and the various tawdry sideshows, all powered by two large steam traction-engines with generators, would have been erected. The fair would then smoulder through the week, breaking into a flaming coal that stood out from the velvet dark in a grand Saturday night finale. By Sunday noon it would have disappeared like a short memory.

Golighty, who managed it, was a big, balding man who had gone to seed in middle age. He smoked cigars, had a paunch, wore shiny pointed boots and when he walked he would lean back into small footsteps like a bass drummer in a marching band. I made a deal with him. As an added attraction, Akil was to give a single performance on the Saturday night.

We advertised on the poster a breathtaking jump over thirty-four barrels. This was true but it didn't mean what people thought it did. The barrels would be stacked two deep. The reality was that he would jump the length of seventeen beer barrels, not remarkable by today's standards, but then again the Norton was hardly leading edge technology.

I rented the barrels from the local brewery and I had got the ramps set up by Thursday morning.

Akil had been hanging around for the past couple of days. There wasn't much that he could do, but I had an inkling that something was different about him, and then it struck me! He usually treated his motorbike as though it were his eldest son. I had not seen Akil tinkering with the Norton.

That was the beginning. At my frequent hints that he should practice a trial run with fewer barrels, he just shrugged. I had never known him like this. Golightly wanted to see what he was getting for his money and was becoming impatient. I had to keep fobbing him off with fibs about teething troubles with the Norton. I assured him that everything would be fine for Saturday, but I did not feel as confident as I had to sound.

Have you ever been in a situation in which everybody knows what is going on except you? Perhaps Akil planned it that way. I might never have found out had I not wandered around the far side of the tip on the Friday afternoon to have a pee. There was no doubt as to what they had been doing. After that, I seemed to run into them everywhere. They couldn't keep their hands off each other.

Their passion was not so much of intensity as of a balance of reciprocity. I had seen the girl before. She was little more than a kid, wore pink tights and did leg kicks in front of the funhouse as the barker beat the drum. Reacting like a Pavlov dog, she performed as though her mind were somewhere else giving no sign that she even knew the audience was there. Her hair was jet and her makeup was caked over a threshold of oyster grey which gave her complexion the, not unattractive, buffered pink of Botswana agate.

Word had it that she was one of Golightly's girls. "For Chrise-sake! go easy," I said. "We don't want trouble with Golightly." As usual, Akil just shrugged.

Even these days, I can feel a quickening at the reminiscence of those fairs. The town's anticipation of the week was primed, like Vesuvius, to gloriously cascade on Saturday night. The mawkish colours bathed in yellows of ambient light as the last of the day drained its Prussian blue from the ink of the blue-black sky. In the confusion of sight and sound, the determined drone of the steam traction engines sounded a bass to the shrill disharmonies of several calliopes. The pungent smell of ozone was triggered by the copper, making and breaking the sizzling voltages. I would glory in the overload of my senses as though I were at the epicentre of a beating heart.

The ramps and barrels were set up on a moderately flat field behind the main fairground. It wasn't exactly an arena, but two areas on either side of the row of barrels roped off for the spectators who were now arriving in tens and twenties, formed an elongated oval. Three hundred feet from the takeoff ramp, and in alignment, they had set up for us a small marquee leaving off the front and back canvasses. Akil was to ride the bike some four hundred yards to the top of the slag, turn and come down the hill gathering the necessary momentum, pass through the marquee, and on to the takeoff ramp.

I found him at the top of the tip by following the smell of oil and petrol. He was sitting on the slag in black leathers, knees pulled up to his chest and his arms wrapped around himself. I had never seen him like this. Beads of sweat stood out on his face. He was in a funk, as scared as you or I would be at the thought of trying such a crazy stunt. I could not get any reason out of him. He was rambling.

I couldn't make sense of a word he said.

I knew it was no use arguing with him and besides, I wasn't going to talk him into anything. I remembered only too well what had happened over at the pithead.

It was obvious to me he was not going to ride that night and so I walked slowly back down the tip to the gathering crowds, trying to figure out what I was going to tell Golightly who was on the opposite side of the grounds waiting at the microphone. It must have taken me all of seven or eight minutes to get down there, when I heard the abrupt roar of the Norton. The baroom,

baroom, as Akil brought it up to temperature, followed by Golightly's dark-brown voice coming across the loudspeakers. "Ladies and Gentlemen... " it said, and then monotone'd into the usual hype.

After an agony of waiting, somewhere in the blackness the bike was gathering speed. He was going too damned fast, I thought.

Why was he travelling at such an insane speed? Then he shot into the floodlights and I knew why. On the pillion was the girl.

Thoughts are occasionally delayed but feelings are instantaneous. I knew what I should have been thinking: it was unlikely that Akil would make the span. It was longer than he had ever tried before and he had not even rehearsed. If he could do it with an extra ninety pounds hanging off the back it would be a miracle.

But that is not what I did think.

As though my mind took its cue from the brilliant focus of light in that eternity of dark, I knew that this was not about Akil or me or the girl or Golightly or tribal customs that robbed men of their souls. It was more fundamental. It was about destiny. We had given fate the opportunity to demonstrate its absolute domination over us.

He hit the ramp doing at least eighty-five. As it took off, the bike stood on its end and wavered across the barrels like a dolphin tail-walking across the surface of a water wonderland. It did not quite make the down slope of the landing ramp, which probably saved them for they would certainly have back-flipped. The rear wheel hit the front edge and that brought the front wheel down, and after a precarious wobble, when it looked as if the bike might slide sideways, Akil pulled it down onto the cinders and out of the splash of light.

The crowd ooh'ed, gasped, roared and broke into a smattering of applause before settling back into an expectant, subdued, babbling as they waited for Akil to take his bow.

I knew he would never return; it was all over. I could hear the laboured pot-pot-pot-pot as the Norton pulled them up on to Brierley Hill and away into the night.

Asylum

I believe they moved me during one of my blackouts.

I have had blackouts since I was a child. Sometimes I would go for days fighting them but I would eventually succumb and go into a *semi-coma*. This happened with such regularity that my parents would put me to bed every night so I would not fall and hurt myself. The blackouts lasted about eight hours and so by morning I would be normal again. I remember strange dreams; at least I thought them strange. But now, they are by no means as peculiar as the reality around me.

Yes, I believe they moved me during one of my blackouts.

At first, I did not realize I was in an institution. There are no walls as I might have expected. We are free to come and go as we wish, though to move between other asylums we need papers. Only gradually did it come to me that I was amongst madness. Every day somebody is knifed, shot or bludgeoned. Sometimes people spontaneously explode, taking others with them. The idea is to kill people to stop them from killing other people.

Curiously, no one thinks that he is John the Baptist or that she is Joan of Arc. Though a number of men think they have the ear of, and are, the right hand man of God, as though God has many right hands. One wonders if God knows? But it is more complicated, for there are many gods and their followers fight amongst themselves in their honour. The land a man stands on is also considered to be sacred, and this he will fight for.

Another astonishing game pits man against man based on superficiality of appearance. Or based upon what his ancestors might have done. Great violence is generated, for we have access to all the latest technologies. This I find difficult to understand. It is no way to run an asylum.

Through the insanity of these games men attempt to prove their sanity. Who do they have to convince but themselves? That is the problem!

For the most part, those of us in the better asylums are kindly treated. There is food, which is available to us in exchange for tokens and notes and tiny pieces of plastic. The plastic is magical, for it merely transfers the potential for work done or work to be done. These can also be used for housing and other necessities and even for pleasures. To acquire these tokens we are required to carry out a variety of tasks for parts of our days. Some inmates are denied the opportunity to do this work. I do not understand why. They are not a whit less insane than the rest of us. Their lot is sad. They are required to beg, and the conditions under which they survive are pitiful; many live in cardboard boxes.

Enormous energy is spent on persuading us all to acquire more goods. This in some way results in more notes, more tokens, more pieces of plastic. Some are burdened with so much that there is hardly room for them to live in their houses, and so large holes are dug under them for storage. Many are in the grip of psychotic compulsions; having worked for more than enough notes and tokens for food and housing and pleasure, they cannot rest. Still they work harder to amass even more. They spend the time in the feeble-mindedness of trading tokens and notes for tokens and notes. It is pitiful to see the looks of blissful idiocy when they increase their holdings. Huge buildings house this game, which has many rituals, such as applauding and ringing of bells. People who amass huge amounts of tokens and notes are greatly honoured, for it is almost criminal to live in cardboard boxes.

Others, who are given somewhat lower standing, though not as low as those who live in cardboard boxes, purchase small pieces of paper on which there are numbers. The numbers are not an indication of quantity as is usual, but merely to indicate a difference. Then one of the pieces of paper is chosen entirely on the basis of unlikelihood. It is as if God had chosen, and that individual, however much he would like to work, is often excused from work for the rest of his life. The other several million people, who received nothing, do not seem to be dissuaded from buying more. It would seem that but a single piece of paper stands between the perpetrations of a fraud sanctioned by society.

Still others have different compulsions. Some run. They call it jogging and it is usually run in wide circles. They do this even though there are machines that compact space, so that wherever a runner stops, he is always where he started. At first I found jogging difficult to understand. If you are going nowhere, then coming back, why not stay where you are? But then I realized it was a kind of flagellation. Joggers are like people in the Middle Ages who curried favour with God in time of plague by dragging heavy crosses and whipping themselves. Jogging is the means of bargaining with God for a longer life. It makes perfect sense.

One man thinks the institution is a giant ball rolling around a star. How can that be? Everyone knows a star has points. Another thinks all straight lines curve. Yesterday I met a woman who thought a pound of lead weighed the same as a pound of feathers. Yet another thinks it possible to travel forwards in time, which of course, is possible as long as you don't think of the past as going backwards.

In the institution, we are encouraged to elevate ourselves, to put intellectual space between ourselves and others. There is a kind of admiration given to those who are able to demonstrate that others are inferior to them. This is done by convincing the few, so the many will follow.

We are well informed by a plethora of laundry marks on wads of white paper, the kind once used for wrapping fish and chips, and which most can decipher. They tell of happenings in other places. There are also boxes with windows to other places, and even to other times, so that the instant between the future and the past is sometimes illusory. They talk to us of accidents, killings and other atrocities. We are encouraged to empathize with the victims though we have never met them. This, I believe to be therapy, a means of preventing us from becoming hardened to violence.

The windows also remind us again and again that something terrible will happen if we don't acquire more things than we need. Other window boxes enable us to communicate by writing on each other's windows as though each were a synapse in a giant mind. There are also small plastic devices that enable us to talk to people who are far away. It is like shouting over long distances. The habit of moving sound around would give the impression to a perfect stranger that everyone is talking to himself and is suffering from earache. Much of this has to do with the pressure on us all to know everything, which fills all time and space with noise. Myth has it that there exists the sound of silence, though I have never heard it.

Sex is used for all kinds of purposes, even occasionally for procreation, though it is much more popular for killing time when there is nothing of much interest on the window boxes. It is also packaged for men who don't know any women, and occasionally packaged for women who don't know any men, or any number of other permutations.

It occurs to me that before they brought me here, my old world was like a woman without makeup. Here in the institution they exaggerate everything. The colours are brighter. There are parks with themes, mountains, castles, wild animals, all designed to be better and more interesting than the real thing, even simulated wars where we might kill people with dabs of paint. We are constantly in the process of trying to outdo God. In one of the wards an inmate may visit a bridge built slightly under the surface of a remote sea, so that he may appear to walk upon the water. Nearby, a vending machine changes water to wine.

Some try to convince the others that the world is getting warmer. The others, in the absence of absolute proof that it is, prefer to bask in the absolute certainty that it isn't.

Though we are always driven to be doing something, a St.Vitus's dance to perform, even those who watch the grasses grow cannot rest until they know the names the blades go by. We may never idle or rest for long. However absurd or illogical the things we do, there is an unspoken agreement to agree to make sense of it. That is what the words are for!

My doctors tell me my illness is complex. They tell me I am out of touch. You must not believe what you see, they tell me. Take heed only of words, for that is where reality lies. That is why I am in the institution. For I have lost the ability to see the relationship of words to reality.

I have made some progress. I used to think the problem was in what people did. Now I know the problem is in what they say.

Listen to your politicians; they are your reality. Do not confuse what you see with what they say, my doctors tell me. Practice, practice, practice words and so...

I wrote:
>There is a part of me
>Which must inform another part of me.
>If it's deceived, which part am I?

I wrote:
>As a child I was reconciled
>To the concept of infinity.
>Then I learned to count from one to ten
>And never comprehended infinity again.

I wrote:
>When of every other loch I know less
>How come I know so much about Loch Ness
>On account of something that might not exist?
>It makes me wonder just what else I've missed?

I wrote:
>How many times have you heard the line,
>"Oh my Lord, is that the time?"
>As though experience needs revision
>To keep in step with a clock's precision.

I wrote:
>Most of us like curly hair
>All of us are intrigued by a spiral stair
>Could it be in some other way
>We are influenced by our DNA?

I wrote:
> Sometimes a wild thought comes to me
> That makes a bargain with reality
> Enough to set my senses reeling
> I should have left it as a feeling

But I am doomed. For it seems to me, that only if everyone stopped, everyone stopped doing everything and saying anything would the blanket of sanity descend upon us all. And that is madness.

Sometimes my doctor asks me questions. "Tell me about the sun," he will say.

"It is my eye's projection in the service of the seasons. Winter is its jailer," I answer.

"... and the moon?"

"Sometimes there is not enough darkness in the night to cover the whole sky."

"Then how do you account for tides?"

"It is the sponges breathing," I reply, and he seems satisfied.

Kafka's Great-Great-Great-Grandson

I suppose there are many people who have physical abnormalities they would sooner not talk about—amusing idiosyncrasies, which, if revealed, might change their friends' attitudes towards them. I would not mention my own peculiarity, for fear some might find it amusing, were it not for a recent and somewhat unsettling further development.

Since I was a boy I have never liked broccoli. I realize anything good for you has to taste awful, but broccoli takes this trend to unacceptable extremes. So it might have been a surprise when my wife, one evening at dinner, gave me a helping of broccoli.

I should explain that my wife is on the leading edge of what is good for me. She watches the current health programs on television and reads the health magazines. Consequently, we have a varied diet. We will have yogurt for a week. She will have discovered that yogurt is particularly good for acne, though of course, neither of us has acne or has ever had acne. The next week, yogurt will be off. They will have announced a further study proving too many yogurts lower resistance to dengue fever. Some years ago I had to bury several large sacks of oat-bran in the backyard. She was big on oat-bran. It was touted as a cholesterol reducer. Then later they discovered the whole idea was a big mistake. In fact oat-bran gave most people severe constipation. But you can imagine that our diet was inexplicably varied, and until recently, rich in soya bean. I dreaded the day when some idiot would come up with a study proving a glass of red wine a day was no longer good for us. Though at times, the studies notwithstanding, my wife could be extraordinarily selective.

So the helping of broccoli was not altogether a surprise. The surprise was that I ate it. My wife tends to take offence if I don't eat everything she puts before me. I told her I would much rather suffer the dreaded disease that it was supposed to head off than eat the awful stuff.

The incident went completely out of my mind until several weeks later when I felt a slight irritation on the fleshy part of the inside of my left arm, about three inches down from where the nurse sticks the needle in to draw blood. There were five, minute dots of color. They looked, for all the world, like paint splatters. You know the kind—when the bristles of a paint brush flick and stipple your hand with perfectly round dots the color of the paint. These were green. I tried to scrape them off with my thumbnail. I tried soap. I tried pumice. But whatever they were, they were not going to come off easily. So I forgot about them, figuring they would probably go away by themselves. A day or two later I had cause to notice them again. The dots were now raised above the skin. They looked like green Braille. You might guess, whenever I was by myself, I examined them— sometimes a dozen times a day. Over the next several weeks I watched the dots develop into stalks and the ends of the stalks blossom into dark, vegetable-green blooms. I nibbled an end. It was unmistakably broccoli.

At first I was so fascinated by the outcropping that I never considered the possibility that this might be just the first in a prodigious outbreak—a kind of *chicken-brox* of broccoli, so to speak. In fact, I was fascinated. Though the sprigs never grew to a height of more than two centimetres, there was something distinctly aesthetic about them. I was reminded of those wonderful landscapes that Capability Brown designed for the great houses of England. I would hold out my arm so the early-morning sun would throw its light onto the miniature scene. It had the elegance of a stand of stately elms, its shadow thrown across a field of rather sallow skin.

I have outgoing friends who would have exploited such a peculiarity—would have used it to be the life and soul at parties, for it would have been a fine conversation piece. But I am a shy person of great introspection, and the very thought of such crass exhibitionism mortified me.

For several weeks I was on tenterhooks. I have a vivid imagination, and some of the places that it occurred to me I might have sprouted, were downright embarrassing. Besides I had no wish to spend the rest of my life as a nursery bedding-box for gestating broccoli. But I need not have worried. There were no further outbreaks. And once the novelty wore off I snipped the sprigs off with a pair of nail scissors. I found that by running my electric razor over my arm when I shaved each morning I could keep them as merely five small green dots.

That was several years ago. We continue with our varied diet, and I still eat some of the vegetables I have an aversion to. But so far no health-nut has cast doubts on the wisdom of drinking a glass of red wine a day. But last week the bubble of my tranquility burst.

I was putting on my pajamas when my wife asked, "What on earth is that on the back of your leg?"

"Where?" I said, but I had already seen the telltale green dots on my right calf. "Just paint," I said, shrugging it off.

As soon as I could get away to the bathroom I examined it. Several yellowish-green spots this time. Over the next few weeks, as I expected, they sprouted. It's difficult to get a good look at your calf. From a distance I suspected Brussels sprouts. But yesterday, I managed to get into one of those infernal yoga positions and have a good look at it through a magnifying glass. You know what? I'm ninety percent certain it's rhubarb.

Rufus and Ridley

A play, in one short act,
written in the form of a short story

The setting is a typical lounge or community room in an Old People's Home in a poorer part of the city. It is sparsely furnished with institutional furniture. An old television set with a broken picture tube stands in one corner. Along one wall is a steam radiator, which periodically gurgles throughout the play. There are no windows.

Centre stage, two wooden chairs with arms face square to the audience.

In the chair on the left sits Ridley, a dignified old man neatly dressed except for his slippers, which have fallen off. He sits with his head on his chest and only occasionally raises it to speak a phrase or two of nonsense in a refined, though affected, English accent before lapsing again into reverie.

In the chair to the right sits Rufus, a big man shabbily dressed whose appearance bears the signs of a life that has been principally motivated by temptation.

Both men have their wrists loosely tied to the arms of the chairs with strips of flowered cloth torn from an old dress. The strips of cloth keep them from wandering as effectively as if they were manacled, but something about the way in which the cloth is tied in bows, suggests kindness.

Overall, the scene is dimly lighted with mauve gels except for the chairs that are lighted with soft spots of slightly yellower light of a higher intensity. The two sturdy, upright, wooden chairs, with square arms, the posture of the two men, and the sparse furnishings, give the room the macabre appearance of an execution chamber.

The action plays to a slow tempo. The narrative is frequently spaced by silences.

A nurse's aide breezes through the room, checks the security of their bindings and talks in a patronizing voice as though they were children.

Now you will look after young Mr. Ridley, won't you?

The aide brandishes a finger.

Don't take him rummaging through the garbage again. Do you hear, Mr. Danton? Do you hear?

Rufus shouts after her with exaggerated sarcasm.

Do you hear, Mr. Danton? Do you hear?
It's RUFUS… . R… U… F… U… S.

Rufus talks to himself.

I suppose she couldn't have known that.
Once,
not the once-not-twice once—the not-now-but-then once.
It's all in the way you make the sounds. Never could make the right sounds, not since I was a baby, all burps and farts, me.
Yes, once.
She couldn't have known that once I had three overcoats.
Yes three!

One from the Sally Ann.
One stinking from the clothes left by the river. But you get used to it.
And old Albert Starkman's, poor bastard.
Wore all three of them over a steaming grating.
The feet swaddled in gauze from the dumpster behind the infirmary.
Ah, for a long warm piss on a cold night!
It's the legs, you know.
But they should have let me crawl.
I was an embarrassment, they said.
I can't bend the legs, I told them.
They could let me die on my feet but they couldn't let me live on my knees.
Where do you think you are, Calcutta? they said.
I am only paying homage to life, I said.
Prostrate to every point of the compass.
How can a man be more devout?
They said I cluttered the sidewalk.
That people might trip over me.
They said I was an embarrassment.
Ridley raises his head.
I say, old chap, I must buy you a drink sometime.
Scotch and soda, or do you take your whiskies neat?
His chin falls back onto his chest.
Rufus wriggles his wrist to see if he can free himself, but the rags hold. He continues:
Fit to be tied, they said.
There's a bunch of sounds for you —
He states in clearly defined words.
Fit—to—be—armchair—tied!
Stretches the sound. Exaggerates its hollowness.
A-r-m-c-h-a-i-r
Now there's a sound for you.
I couldn't stop crawling.

It was the legs.
But it wasn't an embarrassment to me.
He looks down at his wrists.
What couldn't I have done with these rags?
It's all in the wrists now.
Helpless as the legs;
Can't bend them.
He talks directly to the audience.
Had to put the hat between my legs; kept me from fainting.
I tied a stick to the brim so I could push it out beyond the feet.
Spare a quarter, Sir? I'd say.
They won't walk over you, you know, not even to give you a dime.
I kept an even dollar, a quarter, a nickel and two cents in the hat—plucks at the heart string. Encourages them.
Useful stuff, string.
Looks down at his wrists again.
But what couldn't I have done with these rags?
Ridley raises his head.
Howzat? Jolly well played Sir, caught at mid-wicket.
Tries to slap the arms of the chair as though applauding. Lets his chin fall back on his chest.
Rufus ignores the interruption.
They said I'd trip people.
The legs wouldn't straighten.
Move on, they'd say, move on
and I'd crawl hard on the knees until the pants wore through.
Don't forget the hat, they said.
It's just the legs, I said.
Nothing wrong with the head it's as good as ever;
and I'd tap my forefinger to my temple;

I could write a diary on the head.
I'd put on the hat and it would hang down the back like a pigtail.
I mean the stick. Hung down the...
They won't walk over you even to give you a dime.
Ridley lifts his chin again momentarily.
Do pass the marmalade, Darling.
Rufus continues:
Yes, the head's as good as ever.
Shrugs his head towards Ridley as if he is giving the old man "the come on".
Not like his—overgrown from ear to ear. Only the well-trodden paths left now; what's left of his habits.
He's in a world of his own that they don't understand, but then, they're not there, are they?
He should have been a politician.
He makes all the right sounds.
Ridley raises his head and looks around but does not appear to see Rufus.
Don't you dare insult my wife, Sir, or you will feel the weight of my stick across your back.
His head drops back on to his chest.
Rufus continues:
You see, it's all in the sounds.
Now, *she* knew how to make the sounds.
Once—again the then-not-now once; the once as in *"upon a time"*
Yes, once—once, she made the sounds of summer-golden days.
The sounds of purple nights filled with fires that hurried the dawn.
Poor and timid as a church mouse, she was, but she said she loved me.
Ah, the scent of her hair. It was Jasmine.
Why didn't I notice the stars?

Ridley raises his head, looks towards Rufus.
    God bless me. Is that the time? Anyone for tennis?
Rufus, ignoring the comment, continues:
    Oh yes, they gave me a fine beginning!
    They taught me Geography—so I could tell where I am.
    History —
    so I would know if I am at the beginning, or in the middle, or at the end, of time.
    But isn't everybody in the middle?
    Sociology was more useful. At least, it told me I didn't fit in anywhere.
    They taught me Science —
    so I might rid the world of miracles.
    Arithmetic —
    so I could count the stars.
    Geometry —
    So I would know the square on the hypotenuse was equal to the sum of the squares on the other two sides diminished by twice the rectangle contained by one of those sides and the projection of the other upon it.
    Algebra—
    so I could state much the same thing, with different sounds.
Adopts a deep forced bass voice.
    "A" squared plus "B" squared minus two "AB".
    English Grammar —
    so I could learn how to make the sounds.
    English Literature —
    so I would know what sounds to make.
He shouts with a chuckle:
    Oh, and I forgot, Physical Education—I learned *that* all by myself.

But it never mattered where I was, or when, there were so few miracles, I never needed a hypotenuse, and I was too busy furthering my physical education ever to notice the stars.
Only the sounds were left.
Ridley again raises his head.
Try taking it day by day, old chap.
Rufus turns his head to Ridley. For the first time, it seems they are conversing with each other.
Then why do I force myself to lie awake at nights for fear I shall miss the remnants of my days?
They don't tell you that once you have learned to make the sounds there are too many sounds to make.
They told me to be myself, you see. That was the mistake they made.
All my life I have been myself, shitting, belching, farting with a mind filled for a lifetime with the bodies of naked women.
I should have been like Ridley: house-trained, garden-trained, street-trained, city-trained, country-trained, world-trained and potty-trained.
Ridley lost himself in early childhood, became the victim of careful actions and pleasant words. He could never return to who he really was.
Rufus looks towards Ridley as a dark stain spreads down Ridley's trouser leg then he turns towards the audience.
Well, look at that, Ridley's pissed himself. Maybe there is hope yet?
No. No. Rufus as the child is Rufus as the man. Crude. Crude. Crude.
Rufus speaks directly to the audience.

How old were you, and you, and you *(he points with a finger of his restricted hand)* before you surrendered to the comedian?

How old, before you joined the masquerade, before the mime betrayed the voice of your childhood—how old, before you were lost in the mummery of the mind, became an addict of the clichés of a world, whose earth beneath your feet you could not feel, whose skies you could no longer touch—how old? What treasures did you leave in kindergarten? What sacrifices did you make at the altar of adolescence? Have you left the *real you* with the child? Are you now a player of parts?

Rufus is Rufus. You are the players. I am *your* audience

Ridley's head falls back on his chest. Rufus begins to rock his chair from side to side.

I could topple this chair if I tried.
I could crawl like an armchair-turtle.
I could be an endangered species.
I could be the last of my species.
I could scuttle across the golden sand into a silver sea.
Scuttle across the golden sand. I would like that.
Drift in the silver sea—how pleasant the sounds.
He stops rocking, and sighs.
But I would be an embarrassment to them.
Ridley raises his head for the last time.
Is it midnight yet, My Dear?
The stage lights are dimmed even more until only Rufus is softly highlighted in an ambience of crepuscular gloom. The radiator gurgles for the last time. Ridley begins to snore softly. Rufus stares. After half

a minute, he turns his head examining the floor, the walls, the ceiling, as though this were the first time that he had considered his surroundings. He fixes his gaze on a point over the audience and slightly to his right.

Yes, that was it, Jasmine—Jasmine was her name.
He pauses and turns his head slightly to his left.

... or was that her perfume?
He stares vacantly into space as, slowly, the curtain falls.

Affairs of a Welsh Town

The name gave no hint of the town's character, slate-grey hills to the east, grey seas to the west. Known in Roman times for its lead and silver, it made its move at the century's turn. A lavish railway hotel, now the University, was intended to elevate it to a premier holiday seaside town, but the area grew old before its time, perhaps because of its drab shingled beaches and a propensity for rain. In the minds of children, shingle is no substitute for sand even on the sunniest of days. So the town was left with a melancholy, throwing its weight behind sadness.

A shortage of prepared tables threw them together over breakfast. She was the age where a woman fears for her attractiveness. He was approaching the age where life is no longer an expectation but a privilege. They talked of imminent trivia, though not so trivial as the weather. "I'm at loose ends for a couple of days," he told her. "My travel companion, an old acquaintance, has left for Heathrow and the flight back to South Africa. I am leaving for Toronto on Tuesday."

"I would like to stay an extra day," she said, "but with the weekend coming up, my room is no longer available."

He was astonished to hear himself say, "There are two beds in my room. One of them is yours if you wish." He was surprised he had the courage, though he knew that at his age, women were not so much women as they once were, and men were not so much men, including himself. Curiously, the weakening of sexuality brought the sexes closer together. Before they had finished their toast and marmalade, she had agreed. At this, he was not surprised for he recognized the unfettered impetus of loneliness. "I will speak to the manager," he said.

An hour later he helped her move her luggage, one large suitcase with which they both struggled. He could understand her reluctance to move.

His room fronted onto the promenade, a shabby hotel but with the charm of the patina of time. One wall was a large bay window. In hotels, he lived out of a suitcase. There was security in knowing everything was in one place. She was different. At least half of her suitcase was filled with knick-knacks, mostly china, which she arranged about the room as though she were staying forever. Her clothes she folded carefully, putting them in drawers or on coat hangers. One exquisite bone china figurine, somewhat larger than the others, of a girl in a crinoline, she placed studiously in the center of the chest of drawers. He knew little of the value of figurines, but it looked priceless.

The funicular was down and so they climbed Constitution Hill to the Camera Obscura. In the darkened room they turned the lens and looked down on to detailed images of roofs. They were projected magically on the table before them, the purity of light through simple glass of an antique technology giving an intimacy with the town that made them feel as though they were birds in flight.

They walked the promenade against a picket fence of tired hotels, past the band shell, past the faded grandeur of the Railway Inn. They walked past the pier with its cacophony of pin-table sound, past the cairn-worn castle to the lubber'd harbor, its massive trunnion, its blocks of ponderous stone set against the fitful temper of the sea.

That evening they ate late in his room at a low table in the bay window overlooking a darkening sea. They ate

Welsh cheddar, brie, stilton and black olives on sweet buttered new bread, over a Burgundy. She was married, she said, to a man of social distinction, in a market town south of London. She had caught him flagrant in his latest infidelity, packed her suitcase and taken the first train west, wherever it was going. Perhaps it was the wine that placed his hand on hers, her head upon his shoulder, his arm about her. Perhaps it was the wine that touched his fingers to her breast. Through the night, the otiose sea, as though attempting to usurp the land, heaved constantly its way upon the beach, turn and turn about, to slip-slide back down footloose shingles.

She packed with circumspection, wrapping each of the figurines in linen napkins. Of the larger figure, the girl in the crinoline, she took even greater care. Together they loaded her suitcase into the boot of his rental Fiat.

They took the coast-road under a canopy of Welsh rain before turning eastward through steep-sided valleys flushed with falling streams. Then southwest to Laugharne where they looked out over the estuary, looked out over the *heron priested shore,* from the shed above the boathouse where Dylan Thomas coined the words that lifted him for eternity above the mire of the accustomed. Later they dined on pub-fare, leaving in Thomas's *owl-light.*

They stayed inland at an inn on the main street of a coal-redundant mining town. Carefully, she laid out her bric-a-brac and again the figure of the girl in the crinoline took pride of place in the middle of the dresser.

"I doubt I have the courage to leave him," she said. "He is my livelihood, my social position, my level in all things."

He did not question or advise her; such decisions must be left to time and the deliberations of a deeper consciousness.

Through the quiet of the night they missed the sighing of the sea.

They packed to leave. Again, she meticulously wrapped each piece, but this time with a difference. She set aside the figurine of the girl in the crinoline. He was about to hand it to her. "No, leave it," she said. "Leave it where it is," and with finality, she snapped the catches on the suitcase. He watched her but said nothing.

At the station, he helped her lift the suitcase onto the train.

"You will write?" she said.

He nodded, "And you?"

"Yes," she said.

But he knew she would not; he knew he would not. Some things must be left. Some things are so perfect they must not be spoiled by expectations.

Myth of Myths

I had always heard it said that Cerebrus had spent the first years of his life swimming round and round and round, and now, although his mouth opened and closed rhythmically, he seldom said anything. On the rare occasion when he did, it was to murmur ponderously, "I ponder, I ponder," and then he would go on pondering.

Twice, the Council had commended him. Most recently, for his translation of the hieroglyphics on the watershed that can be observed faintly through the veil of algae. It had puzzled the finest minds for generations. "ACME AQUARIUM FILTRATION AND AERATION CO. INC. MILWAUKEE," it read. Though other scholars were still attempting to establish the significance of "CO." and "INC.", as a result of Cerebrus's studies, the petroglyph was now officially considered to be a message from the Gods.

If Cerebrus was a cold fish, in contrast, Chi-bunkin was at least lukewarm. Like the sound of a black piano key, he had a presence that was never quite in keeping with expectation, as though his calling, whatever it might be, was slightly displaced, giving him the melancholy of a melody in a minor key.

Not to paint too grim a picture he was, in a narrow sense, a romantic. In his good moods he might have been described, in the awful phrase the Gods sometimes use, as "fun loving". But there was also a dark side to him when he would descend into a sombre disposition quite suddenly, like an eventide hastened into darkness by crepuscular cloud.

He had two passions. One was understandable, for Angel was a natural gold and a perfect and curvy 26-80-16—millimetres that is! They were fond of each other and from time to time there was talk of fingerlings. His other passion was the *Legend*, and as the festivals approached Chi-bunkin would become more and more preoccupied. "Come on, Chi," I would say, trying to shake him out of it, "let's go down for some of that gourmet algae off the mollusc." But usually, neither Angel nor I could affect any improvement in his mood until after the telling of the Piscean Legend had taken its privilege.

The first of the festivals came at the time of Many Flowers. Haliburt was savant, our storyteller, and he would gather the school about him in the early morning hours. The Council, the Elders, those of us who held no particular office, the feeders and the fingerlings, would gather around Haliburt as he would stand on the rise of round pebbles off the port bow of the pseudo porcelain wreck of the galleon. He was held in great respect, for he was successor to Dolphinium who was successor to Neptunia, and it was said he was descended from Koi blood.

The onset of Haliburt's oration drifted down upon us like a spinner waft on an impetuous stream. Would it be the telling of *The Saga of the Bloody Piranaic Wars*, the ballad of *The Ancient Marliner,* the sad tale of *The Atlantis Chronicles*, or would his preter-dawn discourse be in a lighter vein—perhaps *The Comedy of the Porpoisettes*? Haliburt drew himself up to his full height and on the tips of his fins and in his cave of a voice, he sounded, "Terranious, divinity of all deserts, majesty of all mountains, father of the fields and of the forests."

Like a captive audience at a musical recital treated to an encore of a tune they can whistle, a spontaneous enthusiasm broke forth in the clapping of fins. It was to be the *Taddeous Progeny,* a favourite of us all and a particular favourite of Chi-bunkin.

The gathering settled and Haliburt picked up the narrative. "Before the Eons of Pisces, before the epoch of the great salting, the earth, the sea and the sky were one. And the Gods fought with the light of vipers through cataracts of fire and the whirlpool winds roared with the thunder of the surf and all things were chaos, for the sea, the sky, and the land were one.

"Upon occasion, the great God, great beyond all names, who ruled over all, cast his mindfulness upon the disorder. 'Enough!' he bellowed and looking down upon the apocalypse, charged his subordinates thus: 'To you Mirronex, I bequeath the breath of life, the dominion of the sun and stars; you shall be master of the clouds and custodian of the rainbow. To you, Terranious, I place in trust all that is unyielding and you shall, within your compass, keep patient vigil upon the nobility of the mountains and lowliness of the plains. Nept, to you I commit the enigma of the deeps. You shall calculate the neap of tides and the oscillation of the waves and in your charge I place the creatures, for the seas shall be the amnious of life.' And the great God, great beyond all names, who ruled over all, cast his staff into the waves and there was life."

Chi-bunkin was rapt, immobile as a petrified log.

Haliburt continued. "A great peace fell across the land, the sea, and the sky. The creatures of the green deep and the earthy shallows prospered. In a solitary inlet where the sea emulates the truculence of the land, and the land, surrendering its aridity, mimics the compliance of the sea, there came in passing, one whose name was

Taddeous. Being of an enquiring nature, he would press the elders. 'Why am I captive of the sea?' And gravely the elders would speak of the will of the great God, great beyond all names, and tell of the trusts of his supernumeraries: Mirronex, Terranious and Nept. They would tell of how the land and the sea and the sky, which once were one, were now three.

"But again and again Taddeous would ask himself, 'Why am I a prisoner of the sea?'

"Oft-times he would swim into the cusp of a wave. Launching himself on the spindrift, and flapping his fins frantically, he would cry, 'I can fly! I can fly!' Then sadly he would fall back into the bosom of the sea. He would ride in the saddle of the tide surfing into the shallows, and burrowing into the mud and paddling his fins furiously, he would cry, 'I am running! I am running!' But the slime choked him and sadly he would return to the bosom of the sea.

"The great God had not overlooked Taddeous. His striving was timely, for the God was troubled by the inequity of the sea, lush with life, and its pre-eminence over the barren land and the empty sky, and seeing Taddeous's pathetic struggling in the mud, he took pity. 'Taddeous,' he said, 'you shall be my emissary. Listen to my command, rest easy and fast for a changing six moons and you shall walk upon the land.' Taddeous ceased his struggles and he lay easy and fasted. Imperceptibly, as six solemn moons gave way to five swaggering suns, so his tail and his fins gave way to extraordinary appendages and as the sea and the land humbled their horizons to the unfolding sky, and the God Mirronex flaunted the daystar for the sixth time, Taddeous walked."

Chi-bunkin was held in a vice of persuasion.

For effect, Haliburt released a thin stream of bubbles that he had cunningly concealed in his gill beforehand, interspersing them with his words so that, somewhat in the manner of an auctioneer, he continued the legend. "The creatures of the shallows looked on in wonder. 'It is a miracle; Taddeous walks on land,' they said, and the words were carried on the wind and on the tide. 'Taddeous walks on land. Taddeous walks on the right hand of the God Terranious,' and soon it was known as far as the emerald deeps where even the sun has no dominion. 'Taddeous walks on land. Taddeous walks on the right hand of Terranious. Taddeous is a God'."

Haliburt warmed to the finale and driven by the intensity of his emotions, he teetered precariously, executed a soft-shoe shuffle, and although frowned upon by the elders, he occasionally let fly with a "Hallelujah! Hallelujah!"

"You are the progenitors of the Gods, my children!" he shouted in rising passion. "You are the progenitors of the Gods!" and spinning on his tail, he waved his fin in a broad starboard sweep until, with their eyes following the compass of his gesture, his audience looked in through the algae'd glass at the dim infinitude of the aquarium of the Gods.

He invariably brought the ending of his story dramatically to its virtuous climax coincident with the flash of dawn. And a flash it was. After two or three unnerving preliminary flickers that suggested it might fail, the sun-slit struck, irradiating us with the brilliance of its omnipotent revelation. With the coming of the light the spell was broken. Haliburt stood almost penitent at the unrestrained ovation, and as the tide of poignancy ebbed, the gathering broke up in two's and three's.

Chi-bunkin was the last to leave.

Cerebrus had unravelled the sun-slit hieroglyphics to, "FLUORESCENT COOL WHITE DELUXE 48 INCH," but the scholars were still debating the significance of the "48" and so, for obvious reasons, the word *sun-slit* was still the preferred term in everyday conversation.

This was the most beautiful time of day as it emerged in sudden contrast to the umbra of night. I revelled in sheer delight at the translucent fluorescence that touched with ultramarine the waving fronds of the polyethylene water iris, tinting the upwardness of everything until it mirrored the sky. Even in the grotto, where the stones defied the light, it triumphed, enlisting adjacent surfaces to its purpose until the inner caves were bathed in shimmering indigo reflections. In my wonderment, I was permeated with the tranquillity of summer-limpid pools and the mysteries of ancient seas.

None of the loveliness of our surroundings made the slightest impression upon Chi-bunkin. I was to realise that his spirit was spawned remote upon some other world, consecrated in the gravel of an Elysium stream, and that it was his destiny to brook the falls of scepticism and the crosscurrents of misgiving to effect its homing.

If Haliburt were to be believed, it gave me a warm feeling to think that we had given the Gods a good send-off. But it was my opinion, after watching them for many years looking out at us without a glimmer of expression, that they lacked an essential component of intelligence. I wondered what they thought about all day as they would come and go, moithering like seahorses, drifting in and out of the receding gloom.

"Do you suppose Taddeous was the only one?" said Chi-bunkin, some days after the readings.

We were bottom feeding at the time and I was not keen to engage in a theological argument with him. "You mean the only one to leave the water?" I said. "Can't say I have ever given it much thought," which was true. I would forget about these stories almost as soon as Haliburt had finished telling them.

"There must have been others—after all, there is obviously more than one God," he went on, stopping only to vacuum the algae from another chunk of the resin-coated gravel before expelling it, bee-like, from his tulip lips.

Later I was to learn that he had entered into similar conversations with others. Later I was to realise that, after the telling of the Taddeous legend, there was a part of Chi-bunkin's soul—a fragment of his here-and-now, that was irretrievably left floundering upon that desolate primeval shore. How very clear things are in retrospect.

Angel was the first to notice. She came to me visibly upset. "He's gone!" she said. "It's no use looking. I have searched everywhere. He's gone."

"Nonsense! He must be around somewhere," I said. I took her by the fin and we searched systematically, carefully looking in all his favourite spots. But he was not in the labyrinth of the grotto, nor the hold of the pseudo porcelain shipwreck, nor in the Elders' lagoon. Nobody had seen him since late the day before. Angel was right. Chi-bunkin was gone.

"I knew it! I knew it!" she said. "I couldn't talk any sense into him. He kept telling me that the great God was calling him." I tried to comfort her, but like the quell of windblown sands, a pall of sadness steadily descended upon us.

In the hours that followed, the Council completed its investigation. They discovered a gap slightly nor'west of the watershed, barely large enough, but Chi-bunkin, in good physical shape (I would often see him working out with the barbels) could have easily leapt through. Bloater, a feeder, had observed him a day or two before, engaged in several peculiar callisthenics. He was swimming an inch or two above the gravel bed, then with flailing fins and a late tail-flick—as Bloater put it so picturesquely, "he levitated as though he were on the burp of a trout." This evidence confirmed our suspicions and it became even more obvious when Cerebrus later discovered a message in the sand. Written in the elegant fin of Chi-bunkin it read simply, "Gone to the Gods." It was signed with a flourishing "C".

In the days following, almost imperceptibly, the mood of dejection started to lift, to be gradually replaced by a curiosity until, by the sixth day, the attention of everybody was focused on the aquarium of the Gods. We would watch them come and go, peering out at us with their vacant faces. I suppose we were watching for a sign. "It is so difficult," said Angel, sadly. "They all look alike." She was right of course, but suddenly one appeared whose deportment was familiar. Chi-bunkin had a habit of tilting his head to port in a short, sharp gesture of come-hither as though it were hinged at his gill. One of the Gods had an identical tic. Angel had noticed it too. "It's him! It's him!" she screamed, and in sudden abandon, she lapsed into a cheeky little bubble dance that raised the eyebrows of one or two of the matrons.

Like an infection, the cry spread and soon everybody from the fingerlings to the Council was saying, "It's him! It's him! It's Chi-bunkin!"

The Elders too, could scarcely contain their pleasure, and even Cerebrus could be seen mouthing the words, "It's him."

And so fragments of truth, held together by a desperate communal need to believe, had brought forth a revelation. The question was—were all the pieces from the same puzzle?

Although we looked for days and weeks, none of us ever saw him again.

Gradually, our thoughts of Chi-bunkin were blanketed by the utility of our lives. His memory was supplanted by present routine, passing joy, and sometimes, prolonged sorrows. On the glass near the thermometer, Cerebrus had discovered yet more hieroglyphics. So far, he had deciphered "PLEXI", which he thought was derived from a word in the aquarian runes "plexus" which meant "solar" or "sun". Angel had chosen an eligible young fellow from her coterie of admirers. There was again talk of fingerlings. Haliburt told the telling of the Piscean Legend at the time of Winter Snows. The sun-slit plied its abrupt darks and its hesitant lights with the precision of the Gods, and the scenery of the world continued to pass us by as though buoyed upon a slow moving current.

And so it was, the festival of Many Flowers came around again. It was the last of the Piscean Legends. The onset of Haliburt's oration drifted down upon us like a spinner waft on an impetuous stream. Would it be the telling of *The Sargassian Saga, The Ides of the Prudent Octopii*, the sad tale of *The Mer-Maidens*, or would his preter-dawn discourse be in a lighter vein—perhaps *The Trout Quintets*?

As usual, Haliburt drew himself up to his full height and on the tips of his fins and in his cave of a voice, he sounded, "Chi-bunkin: custodian of the shores and shallows, God of all the fens and marshes, warden of the wetland. Chi-bunkin!" Haliburt triumphed.

As the Legend unfolded, in the certainty of its incidentals, the name Chi-bunkin, Chi-bunkin, Chi-bunkin, fell upon the gathering like summer rain, and from the ambiguity of speculation, the uncertainty of presumption, and the potency of intuition, there germinated a new belief.

The Council looked on with expressions of official satisfaction. The Elders nodded in formal approbation. The rank and file intimated their acquiescence by talking softly amongst themselves. The feeders edged closer to Haliburt. The fingerlings subdued their darts and dashes in keeping with the solemnity of the occasion, and Angel shed a single tear.

Smithereens of wonder had come together through the unravelling of time to form a great truth, but was it a truth the pedigree of which was the mongrel of fancy—a rationale that was no more than the formal pattern of an unexpected order in the chaos of the imagination?

As we settled back comfortably into the ever yielding marshmallow of acceptance, I knew Chi-bunkin would be remembered forever.

Carnations and Reincarnations

Frequently, I wake around 5 a.m. It is when I do the headwork for my writing. Once, a woman in a pink negligee was standing at the foot of the bed. "Come, *mon cheri*," she whispered in a delightful Parisian accent. "Come, let's go for a walk."

"In my pajamas?" I whispered back.

"Don't be silly, nobody's about at this hour," and taking me by the arm she led me down a garden path, and somehow, we found ourselves bathed in warm sunlight.

"Where are we?" I asked.

"The Hanging Gardens of Babylon," she replied.

"I'd expected them to be more impressive than this. They are hardly bigger than a Garden Centre. Are all the other Wonders of the World as crummy as this?"

"None of them can hold a candle to Disney," she said.

From her elegant bearing, I could tell she was a woman of fine breeding; a little dumpy and a year or two beyond her prime perhaps, but still attractive. Her hair was longer than I expected (after I found out who she was), and coiled high in a stylish coif not unlike a swirl of soft ice cream. In the crook of her arm she held several bulging file folders. But for these, and the tag hanging from the hem of her negligee which read Spraul-Mart $8.95, she would have looked perfectly in place on the frieze of a Greek vase. She was courteous in the manner of a government employee who is constantly harassed yet everlastingly conscientious.

"Who are you?" I asked.

"I am your muse. George Sand is the name."

"Not *the* George Sand, the notorious writer George Sand, the women's liberation George Sand, the Frederick Chopin George Sand?"

"One and the same; you are talking to Mme. Chopin, more or less," she said. "You may call me Amantine."

"I thought you always went around in men's clothes," I said.

"I did, but there is not much point these days. People can't tell the difference. Besides, I spend so much of my time in men's bedrooms a negligee is more appropriate."

I gave her a quizzical look. "What exactly do you do?"

"I told you, I am your muse. I compose everything you write. You merely have to show the inclination."

I was relieved. I thought for a moment she might have wanted me for my body. But I continued, "Everything I write? You mean that you are responsible for all the drivel I have ever written? Are you telling me that you caused that hassle over my schoolboy essay about the phallic symbol?"

"Sorry about that," she said. "A bunch of us couldn't wait to see the expression on your prig of an English Master's face. But we can't all be geniuses you know; you're all on the Bell Curve, and it is a matter of supply and demand—the amount of space available for bookstores, and a sufficiency of library shelves."

I was annoyed. After thirty years I still cringe at the thought of that essay. "You might have given a young fellow a hint of what a phallic symbol was," I said. "You almost got me expelled. And what's all this about 'a bunch of you'? You mean there're more than just you?"

"Oh yes, everybody has a muse and every muse has a stable of writers or whatever. Every man has a woman for a muse and a woman's muse is always a man. It is the way it has been since Affirmative Action."

"What if the writer is two-spirited?"

"Then they would have a two-spirited muse."

My dreams never have structure or plots; they are like a film made of old cuttings from the floor of Hollywood editing rooms. This couldn't be a dream. I wondered about the Spraul-Mart tag and her dirty feet. It looked as though she had not washed them in weeks, and although they might not have been noticed on the frieze of a Greek vase, I felt I had a right to a certain standard of personal hygiene from my muse. But thinking it would be rude to comment, I continued. "About this stable of yours, how many other writers am I sharing you with?"

"Well, there was John and Martin—Irving and Amis, that is. There was Gore and Mordecai and Pierre and Farley and Albert Farnsbarns and..."

"Albert Farnsbarns," I interrupted. "Who the heck is Albert Farnsbarns?"

"Yes," she said with a sigh. "I have neglected some of you. It has not been easy giving everybody a fair shake since the cut-backs, but Albert has written some fine obituaries."

I began to feel envious; the obituaries I write always give the impression the deceased should have kicked the bucket years ago. I changed the subject. "You have an interesting job. Do you suppose when I er... you know... when I come over to the other side, that I could be a muse?"

"You could, but I wouldn't recommend it. We are all terribly overworked. I am lucky; I have a brace of novelists, but one of my friends, Tom Hardy—you may have heard of him—has all gossip columnists and people who write cookbooks. Or can you imagine writing advertising copy, or even worse, TV sitcoms for the rest of eternity? We lost quite a number to the Yellow Pages. The P.R. is a pain too. Some of my authors are a terror to deal with. Take e. e. cummings for instance. I once serviced him. He could never keep his nouns separate from his verbs, his adjectives from his adverbs, let alone his *what of a which of a much which,* and once the capitals went out on his typewriter, he was impossible."

"I see what you mean."

"You would be better going into A.I.," she added. "There is more future in it."

"I'll remember that. Look, I could use a bit of help myself right now; I'm thinking of writing a novel. But take it easy on the phallic symbols. A fellow of my age can very easily get the reputation of a dirty old man."

"I know what you mean. I made that mistake with Sam Clemens in his dotage. I will never do that again; for a time there I had to go back to wearing men's clothes. Pity my friend Emily who drew Henry Miller! But I thought it about time you wrote a novel. It's the reason I dropped by. Don't worry," she said, "I'll see what I can do for you. How about something along the lines of the altitude disadvantaged?"

"Not elves again," I moaned.

"I'll put a new spin on them," she promised. "But I must go. Martin's in trouble with *The Pregnant Widow.* Tootle-loo; it has been very nice meeting you."

"Likewise, I'm sure. Give my regards to Fred. Tell him I *love* his Fantasy Impromptu."

"M. Chopin will be pleased to hear that." She walked backwards down the path through a bed of shabby petunias.

"You did a fine job on *The Apprenticeship of Duddy Kravitz*, Amantine!" I shouted, glad that I had not mentioned the Spraul-Mart tag or her grubby feet.

"Thank you. By the way, the bit about *One giant step for mankind* was mine, too."

"Very impressive; were those your lyrics to *Oh Canada*?"

"Don't insult me," were the last words I heard her say before she disappeared behind a large piece of hanging garden that had become detached. But as the rustling of her footsteps receded through dead marigolds, I was left deep in thought. Besides writing, I had dabbled in watercolours, basket weaving, paper tole and I had once engraved the Lord's Prayer on the head of a pin, or at least the first two lines of it, and now I wondered how much my muses had to do with all this. I could almost feel the strings, and I began to wonder if I was a puppet, or a television set without a channel-changer. Was I the fingertip of a single god, as I had thought, or was I the soul of a thousand gods? I stood there in ignorance of more questions that I had not thought to ask. Was there a muse for dreamers?

Turning, I walked back along the path and was in bed minutes before the alarm rang to wake us in time to let the dog out.

"You were restless last night," my wife mumbled.

"I was out walking in the Hanging Gardens of Babylon with George Sand," I said.

"You are writing another short story, aren't you?" she asked, giving me that knowing look.

"A novel," I said, "about elves—elves that are euphoria deprived."

"I'll let the dog out for a pee," she sighed.

Moon Song without Words

From the moment she caught the glint of sunlight in his hair she had the sensation of falling. Now, all that was left to them was the agony of slow death at the hands of the Tremplors.

At first she thought of him as a diversion, a plaything, a toy to keep her amused. It was his muscular build and fair, almost blond hair first attracted her. On her daily rides she saw him working under the spans across the gorge. She was careful not to let her entourage guess her interest.

Later she sent a trusted servant to him and a tryst was arranged.

Her demeanour towards him was that of mistress to servant—the Emperor's third daughter to the assistant keeper of the river. Coquettish, she would tease and play coy, never allowing the familiar. Sometimes she would ridicule him. But he had a manner about him which moved her to continue their meeting. Over time the strain of such formality gradually wore upon her. She had not counted on the effect of his physical presence, nor was he a match for the wiles of her womanhood. Soon, in her own time, she thought of him as a man in the way he had always thought of her as a woman. Her restraint gave way to gentle warmth. His fear, at first dwindling to mere deference, relaxed until they enjoyed the familiarity of equals. As the ceremony was lost to indulgence, they treasured the hours they were together.

She had taken thoughtful measures to avoid discovery. None would loiter near the ruin of the old temple house. It was believed spirits were abroad.

They found in each other a fascination, a liking and a companionship. Their similarities and their differences had combined in gentle affection. They complemented each other like the sun and the moon. But neither the sun nor the moon pays homage to the earth, and unnoticed, the mounting fervour of their desires, by small increments, carried them beyond the refuge of prudence.

She came to him at the beckoning of night and lost herself in the intimacy of his caress, and he in her abundant kisses. Night birds fluttered amongst the leaves. Warily the beasts dogged their thirst to the water hole. Big cats prowled the slopes on barely tactile tread, and in the cloistered grasses creatures stirred and the serpent coiled. The earthy night sang on a tremolo of anticipation. Through the open window, beyond the low hills to the west, a full moon failed and in the folly of an early morning dark they slipped the tether of the long night's fancy and tumbled reckless in the valley of consummate delight.

She left him sleeping, kissing him gently on the brow. Then quietly pulling on her shift and wrapping her throw about her, she let herself down the trap from the loft and tiptoed through the dank, decaying, rooms and the mouldering corridors. In the pink lush of dawn, she passed through the coppice-wood to the concealed door in the garden wall. But now, with precarious portent, for she carried within her, wafted upon the capricious winds of fortune, the inscrutable promise of possibility, the unforeseeable issue of their dalliance—an eddy in the tide of life, which could fashion the sands of time.

The days passed slowly in a prickly heat for it would be several moons before the rains.

He worked to reconstruct the irrigation dams, directing his men, driving, urging and sometimes wallowing in the mud to help lever an errant log. As they hurried to finish the sluices before the rains, his workmen found him more demanding than usual.

She began to attend the temple regularly. Perhaps her minions had noticed her temper was a fragment short now and again. It was more difficult to please her, but her life continued in idleness, which she punctuated by slipping away into the quiet darkness of his life whenever they could arrange this safely.

The mind rarely trifles with the unlikely, the scarcely possible, unless the possibility has fatal consequences; then, like the draught distilled from petals of the nightshade, it heightens sensibility. In the beginning, Time gave them no cause for presentiment and they could not bring themselves to give shape to the thought their destiny trembled upon the caprice of his seed. They placed their faith in the benevolence of the Gods. But as the days fell upon one another like dominoes, they gave voice to a concern that hovered, like the feeling in a windowless room, that it is about to rain.

Days passed slowly. The grasses burned to yellow. Life was like a still pool with scarcely a ripple. Not until the first turn around the washerwoman's ankle would there be the suspicion of the serpent.

Days passed slowly turning soil to dust.

One songbird does not make a summer, for once the heavens had touched the earth, fear chastened them. They knew that fate deals her own odds. The off chance of their imprudent wager chivvied in the deeps of always and scant possibility magnified by terrible consequence kept them on edge.

Weeks passed slowly and the harvests were gathered, and in the idle flicker of nights and days an obscure unease became a focussed concern that would illuminate every moment of their waking.

Morning, night, and sometimes noon, when he could slip away unnoticed, he climbed the knoll to the south bearing of the city. From there, he could see the Princess's window; he ached to see a silken scarf, casually displayed, by which she had arranged to free him from the wretchedness of their vigil. One evening he thought he saw her sign in gold and azure, and like a child he ran through the streets, laughing and crying, until he neared her window. But it was only the evening sun playing tricks.

Each time she awoke, for a brief second life assumed its tranquillity, but only until memory retrieved reality. She would fasten the golden chain about her waist to the same link as the morning before, suffering days of discomfort until she was forced to let it out by several links. Then she would begin the ritual over again. One morning the ends of the chain did not meet.

Days passed into weeks and as the mounting weeks became a wall around their disbelief, they realized, in the emptiness of despair, it was the sun that had denied the moon its changing seasons. Within her there had occurred a starburst—the bitter sweetness of life.

Weeks passed with the impatience of the south wind, for now time was running down.

She knew of the Chad woman in the clearing, but dared not trust anyone. Few would chance helping the Emperor's third daughter in a matter of such delicacy. Besides, she could not bear the thought. It was his child. It was their child.

Weeks passed fleetingly, barely touching the events of the passing days. It was as though the sky had descended and was a mere span above their heads.

He would wake in the night on the jagged edge of terror fearing they had come for him. They would say he had defiled her. They would say she had defiled the night sky. The Sun God would demand retribution. He remembered the timbral drums in the temples, rhythm'd with finger bones upon human skin tensioned by human tendons, given while he was still alive, by a man accused of stealing a pig.

The Tremplors knew how to drain a man of his pain. First, there would be the unravelling —the irritants that would chafe his conduits until he was incontinent, the brine he would be forced to drink. There were salves of ivy, of nettles that raised skin so that a man was driven to scratch himself, though the tips of his fingers had been removed.

The Tremplors were diabolical in making the punishment fit the crime. A man who was suspected of looking into the quarters of concubines had small thorns pushed through his eyelids.

He knew he would die not by days but by weeks. He cursed his imagination for he dared not think about what they would do to her and to the child. From then on he could sleep only when the drowse of exhaustion was upon him.

Only her most intimate handmaiden suspected. Although she ate sparingly and wore the most voluminous of her wrappings, she was now forced to bind lengths of muslin tightly about her. As she neared the edge of breakdown, only in the brief, idyllic moments when they lay in each other's arms, could she forget the terror.

He could have run. The assistant river-master often worked in the surrounding villages and would be away for several days. The head start would be risky. The villagers would be terrified of helping him, and out of fear, would co-operate with the authority. The Tremplors' runners and their fray-dogs could track in one day what a man could run in three. Nevertheless, there was a chance. But he could not take her with him and he would not leave her.

For more than a week she had not dared leave her rooms for she had now nurtured his seed for more than five moons.

At last the rains came and the business of the city slowed. The river was no longer navigable. The gorge became a cataract. It was a seven-day trek around the mountain.

Three days after the rains began the Tremplors prepared the great hall for the festival of the sacrifices to the Gods. With the festival came the showing of the young women. For weeks now the needle-workers had been sewing the chiffon, the meshes and the flimsy silks.

The dark held no qualms; no one else this night was beyond the city wall. The men were already well into their cups in celebration of the morrow's festival and the women taken in preparation of the feast.

The timbre of the rain was that of nature's short extravagance, yet it had now poured unabated for three days. Each drop striking the river with a sharp slap became in unison a staccato roar. They were bedraggled in seconds, their flimsy coverings drenched to transparency, worn like a second skin. In the short distance the coracle had floated downriver, water swirled about her feet.

If they were swept safely through the cataract... the Devil's Whirlpool... if they could survive the weeks of lesser rapids downriver... if they could evade the runners to whom the Tremplors would offer reward to follow them... if they could fool the authority into thinking they had perished... if they could evade the hostile tribes... if they did not fall prey to the beasts... if they could make their way north into the hill country... then, under a new moon... perhaps?

They peered with squinting eyes through the singing torrents of rain and floated towards the thunder of the rapids. Talk would not carry over the deafening sound, and walled in the curtain of water, all thought was suspended as though they had been transported into another time, another life.

She could not hear him over the bawl of sound. There was no need for words. There had never been a need for words. Placing his hand gently upon her swollen belly, a lifetime of understanding passed between them.

Robinson Crusoe

A jet was unusual this far south of the regular lanes and this one was in trouble. The pilot was having difficulty staying on course. Suddenly the plane went into a spin, losing height rapidly and pulling out a few hundred feet above the waves. I watched it with detached amusement. No doubt they were trying to crash-land close to the island, on the beach if possible. As it was, they hit the top third of the swell two or three hundred yards beyond the reef. The waves ripped off the engines and within two minutes the plane had disappeared. I made a point of marking the spot. It would be worth a dive. There was a shallow shelf that would have supported what was left of the aircraft. There might be useful parts to scavenge.

Through the glasses I could see four survivors laboriously making their way over the reef into the lagoon. Two of them seemed to be supporting a third. The fourth was a slower swimmer. I could not have helped if I'd wanted to. I was several hundred yards inland, watching from a favourite lookout. It was to avoid intrusions like this that I had left the outside world. Besides, by now they had reached the beach and seemed to be in remarkably good shape considering their ordeal. I would make my way down later, taking care not to be seen. I wanted to take stock of my visitors first.

I should explain myself. To all appearances I am Robinson Crusoe, but that is deceiving. I have lived here, alone, for almost five years now, even though I have the facility to contact the outside world, and could be picked up within a few weeks. But I have no wish to return, finding the world an infuriating and tedious place. I came here because I wanted to be, and am, the master of my own destiny and I don't wish to have this interfered with by the recent happening.

I settled myself in the undergrowth not more than a few yards from them. I learned a lot from watching their behavior. They had had a miraculous escape. Naturally they were in a state of shock, though apparently uninjured, yet they still maintained a previous and absurd attitude to each other that was comical under the circumstances. There were three men and a woman. From what was left of the men's clothes, I could tell that they were "suits". The woman too, had once been smartly dressed, judging from what was left after a brief swim, and some 300 yards of clambering over rough coral. Two of the men and the woman, referred to the third man, respectfully, as Mr. President. He was head of a Western democracy. It's not important which democracy, just that they all spoke English. But I knew this man. Oh my God! I thought to myself. What a stroke of luck.

I guessed that one of the men was a political aide, the other, who still toted a gun in a holster under his arm, probably a bodyguard, and the woman possibly a secretary or a press agent.

This is going to sound like paranoia, but I make no apologies; politics was one of the reasons I got off the real world, and I knew now that three of the visitors would go to any lengths in the interests of the fourth. If I were to be amongst such lengths I wanted it to be on my terms—for I had once been the victim of the ultimate political faith in an icon—and so decided I would leave them to stew in the island juices for a while. In an hour or two when the sun went down, their beach would be alive with ten thousand land crabs. It can be a terrifying place. I know from my first night on the island.

I silently retreated to a place I came upon one day on a difficult climb. It was a network of caves off the vent of an ancient volcano, a place so private, so unapproachable that no one is even remotely likely to find it. I could even light a fire here and they would not suspect.

There were other reasons why I chose not to make myself known to them. If the aircraft had managed to send a mayday communicating their position, then within a few days they would be picked up, resolving my problem. If, on the other hand, they were stranded, that would call for an altogether different strategy, for whether they realized it or not, they would be my prisoners. On no account must the outside world be allowed to upset my equilibrium.

Then I heard shots. Darkness was falling. The land crabs must be making their appearance. Not a good policy, I thought, wasting ammunition. Soon they would need food, and I doubted they could match my skills at hunting wild boar without firearms, or for that matter, shinning up trees. They might need the big man's handgun. I remembered how it had taken me all of two years to develop the "live off the land" skills, and in the meantime I almost starved. My first impression of my four guests was that they were nowhere near as able as I was when I had arrived here. Their skills on the hustings, in the boardrooms, in the half-truth of words, would be of no earthly use to them here.

There is a mythology about South Sea Islands, that they are idyllic. Up to a point that can be so, but there are many hazards and you need a deal of savvy, not to mention luck, if in the beginning, you are not going to be laid low by some of them. I was fortunate and am now able to live in comparative comfort, in harmony with my surroundings and without any of the stress of the so-called civilized world. Observing my recent visitors was going to be an interesting new pastime. I inhabited mainly the other side of the island. Tomorrow, I would make sure my outrigger and few possessions were hidden from sight. Not a big job, since I am always careful not to leave evidence of my presence.

Then I heard more gunshots.

In the beginning, water had been a problem for me. Fortunately, or unfortunately, for them it won't be a problem, at least for the present. Yesterday, I noticed all the signs of the imminent arrival of a tropical storm. By midday tomorrow we shall be in the thick of it. I am well provisioned and shall wait it out in the comfort of my dry and sheltered caves, along with my books.

From time to time over the next three days, I gave a thought to how they might be doing. I presumed they would have had the sense to move to higher ground. With the storm surge, that beach would be under twenty feet of water. They would be fine as long as they didn't do anything stupid. They would be damned uncomfortable of course for there was little or no shelter unless they could make it themselves, and I would not have left them there had they not been politicians... but after what had happened to me...

The island was large enough for me to avoid them forever if necessary. I wondered if they had used up all their ammunition. If not, I would feel more comfortable if I had the gun.

My beef was only with Mr. President. The problem was: what to do with the other three. There was an obvious solution but I'm not in the habit of murdering people, even people who might want to murder me. After the storm abated on the third day, circumstances suggested a solution, though they might need a little help from me.

Just before dark I noticed smoke on the horizon. The pilot of the crashed jet had likely managed to send out a mayday, I thought. The rescue ship, a small merchantman, approached my side of the island. The others would not yet have seen it. It was too dark by the time it anchored offshore. I guessed that they would wait until tomorrow to circle the island looking for signs of life and then perhaps, send a boat ashore. This gave me about six hours to execute my plan.

My visitors had spent the day drying out. They had moved onto higher ground above the land-crab beach. I waited until they were asleep. Luckily for me, Mr. President was sleeping in a crude lean-to that they had made for him, covered with leaves and some distance from where the others slept. I was well trained to silently immobilize a man without killing him. Within seconds, I had him bound and gagged and over my shoulder. I carried him to a place they would never find him, and even if he yelled his lungs out they would never hear him. Stripping him of his clothes, I went down to the land-crab beach, careful to leave a trail of footprints, and left the pile of his neatly folded clothes at the water's edge.

The next morning there was the expected consternation. It wasn't long before the big guy followed the footprints down to the water's edge and found the pile of clothes. My three visitors realized with horror that they had lost their President. There was a lot of splashing around in the lagoon to see if they could find him. The woman ran along the shore in case he might have washed up on another beach, and in the middle of all this there were two long belches from the steamer that had circled the island. My visitors were caught between the joy of finding they were going to be rescued and chagrin of finding they had lost the President.

A ship's boat came ashore. There was the usual shaking of hands, a deal of discussion which I could only guess at, since, with all those people around, I had to back off. Some of the crew dived into the lagoon, but of course they found no sign of the President. Later in the day a warship arrived under the flag of the President's country. On the following day a cruiser and another destroyer arrived. At one point there were as many as a hundred people on the island. Of course I didn't like this, but there was little I could do about it. Although the search parties were organized they found nothing and after a decent time had elapsed so they could say that every effort had been made to find the President, or the President's body, one by one the warships left, taking what remained of the aircraft and the three survivors with them. I could imagine the field day the press must be having.

Once more the island was its usual quiet Eden.

In the meantime I had been making my guest comfortable, for I had plans for him. But first I had to bury all the garbage that loud and uncouth crowd had left. The crews from the ships had left crap everywhere. I dug holes and when I filled them in, left three elongated mounds so it looked as if there were three graves. I finished each of them off with two sticks tied together to look like crude crosses. Then I went back to the cave.

Mr. President still had no idea who I was. I had kept him blindfolded and fed him, mostly on coconut, including the milk that I doctored with an effective soporific made from an herb I discovered on the island. Sometimes I used it myself when I could not sleep, though I preferred my homemade wine or sometimes my moonshine. He had slept soundly, and now it was time to wake him up. The light was poor in the cave and it took him a minute or two to come around, then with a look of astonishment, he said "My God, it's you, Parnell. I thought you were dead!"

"I would have been dead if you had your way. You were a crooked son of a bitch, Ralph, and you know it."

"Look Parnell, I'm sorry about this. It's just they didn't want to take the risk of you blabbing and... "

I cut him short: "It's of no matter. Over. Done with."

He seemed relieved I was not making a big thing of it. Then he said, "Where am I?"

"You are still on the island."

"Then where's Bulkly, Snide, and Miss Deskney?"

"Afraid I had to get rid of them." I had every reason to make him think I could be ruthless.

"My God!" and he put his head in his hands. "Parnell, you swine."

"I think you should address me as Sir or Mr. Parnell," I said, and so ended our first conversation.

At first he balked at calling me Sir or Mister, but after a couple of days, when he got good and hungry, he began to see it from my point of view. Coming across those three "graves" could have had something to do with it.

So, that is how I got my Man Friday. He soon realized that I owned him. Without me he would starve. I feed him, clothe him and keep a roof over his head. I am also his doctor. Given that he was a politician, I was surprised how quickly he learned. I soon had him making soap, doing my cooking and washing, peeling yams, tending the still, bottling the wine, chopping firewood, even sewing and darning, and generally cleaning up after me. He is lousy at chess, but I get him reading to me like that fellow in the short story I once read about a man who got lost in the jungle and spent the rest of his life having to read novels to an ornery native chief. I have a particular fondness for books on left wing politics.

He is competent at most things as long as I don't give him anything to do that needs too much brain power. But on the whole, the idea pleases me, and besides I feel I am doing the world a big favour by keeping him from screwing it up even more. They are still fighting several wars he started.

I reward him with tidbits when he does something particularly well. Just for the hell of it though, I still call him Mr. President.

"Mr. President," I say, "time to dig out the latrine again."

"Yes Sir, Mr. Parnell," he says, and he starts to shovel.

It is the one chore I can give him of which he has had some previous experience.

The Banjo
Dedicated to N.S.

I have a writer friend who is possessed of owls, whales and banjos. In other ways he seems quite normal. I don't know about the owls and whales, they sound distinctly Freudian, but I can sympathize with his obsession with the banjo. It happened to me.

During the depression, my father indulged in the illusion of owning a house. In fact, the bank allowed him to live in it for a short while. When he lost his job, we took in a lodger, actually two lodgers—a man and his wife. The man played the banjo and I must have shown an interest because my parents bought me a toy banjo, though how they afforded it I shall never know.

One day I was left in the care of the lodger and his wife. I heard a banjo playing in the next room. Picking up my own banjo, I timidly peeked around the door. Nobody was more timid than I at the age of four—even mice didn't run away from me. But the banjo player and his wife invited me in.

"Are you hungry?" they asked. I said yes and they gave me a sardine sandwich. The banjo player looked at my banjo. Now we all know the banjo is difficult to listen to, but few realize it is not an easy instrument to play either. My toy banjo was exceptionally difficult because the strings were painted on. The banjo player, immediately realizing the problem, took a matchbox for a bridge and with several rubber bands improved my banjo so that I could play along with him. Later in life I would often ponder how the banjo was ever developed before the advent of the twanging of rubber bands. If I remember rightly, I played the treble while he played the bass line.

For a while I had ambitions to play the music halls. I think this is where my banjo obsession started because ever since, I have had a hankering for sardine sandwiches.

Early one morning the lodgers left, taking with them their furniture and the rent, and their banjo, on a motorbike and sidecar which they slipped into neutral and rolled down the hill until they were out of earshot. But my obsession did not leave with them. It lurked somewhere deep in the recesses of my subconscious along with several perversions, though there were no owls or whales.

I suppose I have always been tethered to the banjo with gossamer strings. I developed a taste for serious music. I would be sitting at the opera listening to Isolde singing of love over the dying Tristan, and at a moment of the most tender passion, in a serendipity of harmonics, I would find myself spirited to some honky-tonk thrilled by that unique timbre of banjo sound, starting with the expected carry of a marimba band and ending disappointingly prematurely with a thump and the annoyance of a drum with a bit of a theremin thrown in. I would be carried on a tremolo of ecstasy listening to the banjo runs up and down the frets, the fascinating sound as though Star War's robot R2D2 was clearing its throat.

It is rare that man goes through life without giving full rein to all his obsessions. It was inevitable that sooner or later, the niggling at the back of my mind would, out of desperation for a bit of peace, drive me into buying a banjo. My first banjo was a cheapie. I mistakenly thought that those small knobs at the far end of the neck were for tensioning the strings, until I found they were for bending the banjo into the shape of a bow. There are shortcomings to a banjo that you must play using only the notes that the manufacturer originally built into the strings. But I did take lessons until my banjo teacher up and died—or should that be down and died? I felt guilty about that.

But I was never much of a banjo player. I couldn't find find music slow enough to play. The banjo is not an instrument suited to dreamy love songs, nor to dirges, nor to requiem. I marveled at real musicians as they discussed last night's hockey game while their fingers played *Flight of the Bumble Bee*, and I, with my attention riveted, was two bars behind before I got to the end of the staff. I concluded that I was a slow thinker—that by the time my thoughts had decided which arm to go down, which finger to tweak, in a manner of speaking, the moment had passed. But, at my best, at the height of my incompetence, playing by myself in an empty house, I was terrific. Fortunately, I think slowly when I'm listening to music too. I must have missed more than half of it.

Somewhere tucked away at my daughter's house is an old Gibson banjo and a pile of sheet music. These days I think even more slowly. I doubt the thoughts would ever get past my shoulder blades before the listener lost interest, but the young covet what the old have lost. I don't regret my short excursion into music. In fact, I kind of enjoyed it. I couldn't have done any better if my obsession had been with owls or whales.

A Black Pebble

It would be an unusual pebble to find on a beach, yet I found it in a mouth. It was black, polished and about the size of a robin's egg. And I found it in his mouth.

I should explain that I work for an undertaker. My job is to prepare the cadavers. This one was a young man about my own age, and by appearances, in excellent physical shape.

My ambition was to become a doctor, perhaps a pathologist, but economics did not allow for it. In the meantime, I had this job at the undertaker's. I still retained that curiosity for what had been the cause of my charge's demise. In this case I could see no evidence of accident or illness. His face was drawn, tired looking, though otherwise he might well have been an athlete.

It was during my usual procedures for preparing the body that I found the pebble under his tongue. I put it to one side and then later, I washed it in a solution of alcohol, and since there was a fascination about it, I put it in my pocket.

I forgot about it for a few days until one evening, just as I was getting ready for bed, I felt its roundness in my pocket. I recall rubbing it between my finger and thumb and within a minute or two I heard a knock on the sliding glass door that led out to the balcony. Naturally I was amazed since my apartment is on the 14th floor. Who would be on a balcony fourteen floors up, especially at this time of night? And how could they possibly have gotten there?

I slipped the catch on the door and before I had time to realize what was happening she was on top of me. What happened then could only be described as utter uninhibited passion. Hour after hour it went on. Neither of us could control ourselves, until a few minutes before dawn, when she left.

The whole event took me by complete surprise that first night, but subsequently, although I cannot say I understand, certain peculiarities have become known to me. For instance, each night, and there have been many since I became addicted to her, she leaves a broomstick leaning against the balcony rail. Witches are folklore, I tell myself—absurdities of the imagination—and never more so than a witch so stunningly beautiful. Granted, she wore the typical hat, wide-brimmed and pointy, her only other attire being: calf-length boots and the briefest of chic, black, undies ornamented by the sexiest of retrospective garters guaranteed to drive any man mad.

After that first night, like the alcoholic desperately trying not to take his first drink, I would find myself unable to resist rubbing the black pebble to summon her to my bed where she would take me to paradise and back ten thousand times. I still could not bring myself to believe she was a witch, though sometimes I would watch her through the blinds as she departed and see her traditional silhouette as she swept in front of the moon.

Total lack of sleep and exhaustion soon caught up with me. My social life began to fray at the edges. I became the mere shadow of my former self. My girlfriend left me. My boss found me, on several occasions, draped over his clients fast asleep. He threatened to fire me. Still I could not help myself. I was utterly dominated by her and subject to her every whim. I was helpless. My health was taking a terrible beating, though my body continued to be infused with her energies through countless nights of irresistible non-stop euphoria. Under her imprecations, for hours at a time, I became super-stud. There is another ominous ritual that puts the fear of heathen gods into me: every morning before she leaves, shortly before dawn and while it is still dark, she leans over me and playfully pops the black pebble into my mouth.

The Bottom Step

The Humane Society took Sandy. They said they would find him a good home. I believe they did. That was when I moved into the room. No pets, Mr. Randle had said.

I could never have imagined that I would end up like this. Me, who had worked all my life! One after the other, so many things happened I could hardly get my breath.

I would have liked kids. But I have always been shy and I suppose I was never a great catch. At least no man seemed to have thought so. There was the thing that George and I had going for a few years, but nothing permanent came of it. Then I had to look after Dad. I thought it would be a job for a month or two, but it turned out to be for six years—until he went into the nursing home shortly before his last illness.

I suppose when I took out the second mortgage on the house it was the beginning of my life's unraveling. Health Care looked after most of the expense, but not all of it. Dad could never convince them he needed a wheelchair, so I had to pay for it myself. Then there were the ramps and modifications. It all added up.

My wages from Fawcetts were barely enough to pay the increased payments, but along with Dad's pension, we managed. Then a conglomerate took over Fawcetts. A machine did most of the work I did, but they kept me on until the new company decided to make all toothbrushes in their parent plant in Alberta. Then for a while I was part-time. It was not a pink slip; Mr. Chapman told me himself. Shortly before lunch one day, he brought me into the office and thanked me for my many years of service. It wasn't up to him, he said. His hands were tied. I thanked him. It wasn't until I got home in the middle of the day that I cried.

For a few months, my severance pay was enough to cover the mortgage. Perhaps I should have sold the house then, for the money didn't last long. But I thought I would get another job, you see. Day after day I scanned the employment lists but little was offered to a 52-year-old woman with minimal skills. At first, out of desperation, I took anything. For a while I was a cleaner, but the hourly rate was so low that I still couldn't keep up the payments. And what's more, while I was working, I could not look for a better job. I tried to get unemployment insurance but they said I must use up the severance money first. Then they said I had not worked recently, and something about the part-time work was such that I did not qualify.

The bank was very nice about it. The manager, Mr. Claybourne, was most upset at losing so loyal a customer. His hands were tied, he said. Foreclosures were always on instructions from Head Office.

For a while I had a little money from the sale of the furniture, but not much. It was then, I moved into the room. I took only Mother's chair with me, the green brocade chair with the soft arms. That is when I took Sandy to the animal shelter. Still I scanned the employment possibilities, but now I doubted that I would ever get a job. I was beginning to run out of tears.

Looking back it seems like small potatoes, but at the time it was terrible. Me, who had never taken a penny from anybody that I couldn't pay back—me, going on welfare! I swallowed my pride, as they say, and at first I managed—just about. Then one day my welfare check was less than usual. I was embarrassed to go to the office but went anyway. There must be some mistake, I said. Look, I told the girl, my rent is almost all of this. There was no mistake, she said, the government had reduced welfare to bring the Province in line with other Provinces. Her hands were tied, she said.

Perhaps right then I should have tried to get a cheaper room in a less respectable district, but there were no cheaper rooms. Mr. Randle said he couldn't reduce the rent. He lived on a small pension himself. His hands were tied, he said.

I knew then, I could not pay the rent and eat. As it was, I lived on pasta and week-old bread. Toast-bread they called it. Mobility was a problem. I could rarely afford bus fare. I walked the six kilometers to the employment office. It meant that I could only shop in the immediate area and I missed out on many of the bargains that the larger food stores offered. Nor could I ever buy anything in quantity. Occasionally I would ration my dollars and cents and take a bus to a food bank but I could only bring back what I could carry. It did help a little. My only extravagance was milk, sugar and tea. Sometimes, when I was really hungry, I would make myself a nice cup of tea.

I had not bought any clothes since I lost my job. Most of what I was wearing was held together by needle and thread, but by now the soles of my shoes were wearing thin. I suppose there were charities to which I could have appealed for help. Embarrassment prevented me. I was afraid to admit to myself that things had reached such a sad state.

I had passed Bob's Café many times. In the window was a sign 'Breakfast of two eggs, bacon, ham or sausage, home fries, toast and coffee $1.99.' One day, I weakened. I shall remember that meal for the rest of my life.

Mr. Randle didn't say anything the first month I was short on the rent. But the next month he told me it could not go on. He lived on a small pension, he said. He had his own mortgage to pay. His hands were tied.

I had never stolen a single thing in my life when I stole the egg. I slipped it slyly out of the carton and into my pocket. I was terrified as I passed through the wicket, but the cashier was not suspicious. I poached the egg on the hot plate the morning I left my room. I ate it together with two rounds of toast and the remains of a jar of marmalade I had foolishly kept for special occasions. I remember clearly the morning I left my room, as I remember all of these incidents. They were all steps in my life. They were all downward steps in my life.

Everything was in two suitcases, one larger than the other. Everything, that is, except Mother's chair that was left to pay off part of Mr. Randle's rent. Once I was out on the sidewalk I realized I had made a mistake. There was no way I could lug the suitcases far. I struggled with them for several hundred meters to a small parkette in which there were children's swings. A few benches surrounded it. In the far corner was a small coppice where children played hide and seek. I dragged the suitcases to the bench under the trees.

I remember the awful feeling of nervousness. I suppose I was frightened. At first, when I lost my job, I had felt alienated from the world. Now I felt severed from it—felt I owed it an apology for being the way I was. Up to now I had hoped that my circumstances were temporary. I had expected I would get another job, expected to keep up the mortgage payments, expected to be able to keep the room, expected to pay Mr. Randle his rent, expected to be able to pay Mrs. Trent for the cans of soup she had kindly given me. I expected that one day, I might be able to afford a small apartment where I might keep another Sandy. One by one these hopes were dashed and as I found myself on the sidewalk that morning I realized I might never again raise myself up. One of the suitcases had to go. I could not carry both and it would be awkward to take them into a café or even a hamburger joint, let alone onto a bus.

I was opening both suitcases, trying to decide which of my things I could afford to leave behind, when I had the feeling of being watched. Turning, I saw a small boy with Down's Syndrome, which probably accounted for why he was not at school. I hurriedly closed the suitcases and waited until his mother called him. After he had gone, I dragged the suitcases back in amongst the trees. I kept the most practical of my clothes, discarding summer dresses and the few fancy things that I owned. This included some fifteen little bottles of scent that my mother had given me when I was a girl, on high days and holidays. I had kept them because of the many pleasant associations. Even so, I figured that I might have to leave more than half of my belongings behind.

I sat in the park all that day. Around seven, I hid the large suitcase in the trees and taking the small one, went across to a café for a coffee and Danish. When I gave Mr. Randle as much of the rent as I had, he refused to take the two $5 bills. In fact, he had hugged me, and then turning quickly, went back into his room. "God bless you, Love," he had mumbled. In the café, I was able to relieve myself before returning to the park bench. In the beginning, finding washrooms was one of my biggest problems. As darkness fell, I slipped quietly into the wood and settled down with my back against a tree. So much for the first day, I thought.

I woke up shivering. It was late May; the nights were cool. Through the trees, I saw the lighted street deserted. It occurred to me how I might take a few more of my belongings with me. I began to put slacks over slacks, and even dresses over slacks, sweaters over sweaters, socks over socks, until I bulged all over and my topcoat would barely fasten. What remained I was able to pack into the small suitcase. I took everything with me except the little bottles of scent which, with the aid of the handle of my hairbrush I buried under a tree. I had a vague idea that one day I might come back for them.

Staying there would have been impossible. I had heard there were places downtown where I might get a meal. Since I had all the time in the world, I decided to walk. Even the smaller suitcase was difficult to carry. I took frequent rests, carrying it in turns with my left, then my right arm. As the sun came up, I began to sweat with all my extra clothes. Then I needed a washroom. I trudged on towards a MacDaniels sign at the far end of a distant stretch of malls.

I ordered a coffee and the MacDaniels equivalent of a Danish and simply sat there. I was in a quandary. Putting on all the clothes was not a good idea. The day was warming up and I was sweltering. Yet if I took them off there was no way I could carry them. The matter was decided for me when a young man, evidently the manager, came up to the table and said, "I'm sorry. You can't sit here all day, Grandma." I knew then that, already, I had left the sanctuary of ordinary people. My bulging all over with extra clothes had given me the appearance that people associated with being a little touched in the head.

I reached the downtown area late in the afternoon, and asked a kindly-looking man the way to the mission. "Straight down here, Love," he pointed. "Second on the left. You can't miss it," and he pressed a loonie into my hand. Before I could refuse it, he had walked off. I lined up with the others and they gave me my first meal. It was plain but good nourishing food. I did not stay at the mission that first night, for I found some of the people rather dirty and smelly, but went to the bus shelter where I sat all night dozing on a bench. Nobody disturbed me. I suppose my suitcase still gave me enough of the appearance of a traveler.

I will not bore you with the details of those first weeks: of how, bewildered and frightened, I stayed at the shelters, and how my last remaining belongings were stolen from me; of how I was rudely rolled off park benches by those who, in the hierarchy of the system, had greater claim to them; of how, for a short time, I shared a room with six women and how I feared for my life when they got into the booze; of how I learned to avoid the youth gangs; of how I learned to recognize the psychos; of how I learned where to get a free meal, where to get a handout, where I could get a tooth removed, where I could find shelter and how long I could stay before they would move me on, where I could find washrooms, where I could get a bath. All this I learned through a hot summer and an Indian fall.

It was fortunate my initiation had not come in winter, for had I been forced to leave earlier or later, I would not have survived.

I suppose I am a private person. I like to distance myself from others. That is very difficult under the circumstances. At any rate, I decided to go it alone. I avoid the shelters except on the coldest nights. The coming winter will be my third. I think I have bottomed out. I believe I have stopped sinking.

There are always kind people. One cold, sleeting February day last year, a man pressed a bill into my hand. Perhaps it's five dollars, I thought, but when I looked it was a hundred-dollar bill. What a godsend! I needed shoes. I needed clothes. I needed everything. But I could not bring myself to spend it on utilities. I set out for

Mimico, to the cheap motels that cater mostly to the sex trade. I decided not to take a streetcar. I walked. Walking is not so bad since I got rid of the suitcase. I carry my things in plastic grocery bags now. All one night I walked through sleet and slush. I was soaked by the time I got there, but for once, I welcomed the discomfort.

I asked the man in the office how long I could stay for fifty dollars? For seconds he looked at me and I thought he was going to say he had no vacancies but then he said, "One night." I gave him the money. He gave me the key. As I left the office he called after me, "Two nights, Love—two nights," and he gave me a slight nod of understanding.

The room was shabby, but to me, it was a palace. I turned up the heat, turned on the television, felt the softness of the mattress, and walking into the bathroom, let hot water run over my hands. That afternoon I crossed the street to the Supermarket, in the luxury of knowing my stuff would not be stolen. I bought shampoo and talcum powder. I bought new bread and cheese and real butter and orange juice and an apple and an orange.

I washed my hair with the scented shampoo, bathed and showered in the hot water and bathed and showered again. That evening I ate the buttered bread and cheese, with the apple and the orange for dessert. Then in the altogether, for the room was gloriously warm, I propped myself up on the bed and watched television. I felt like a young girl again.

I slept in the next morning in the heaven of knowing the washroom was no more than a half-dozen steps away. That evening I ate at a local restaurant. I like liver and onions. Afterwards, I had apple pie for dessert. As the waitress filled my cup with coffee for the third time, I relished the thought that, when I left the restaurant, if only for an evening, I would be going back to somewhere

where I belonged. Home is not a mere construction of bricks on a nondescript street. Home is a tether in the mind—a sailor's star around which a life orbits. Home is a place of love. Without it I am always lost, and one direction is as good as another.

Nobody could work as hard at a job as I have to work to survive. I am a gerbil on a treadmill of endless drudgery—a treadmill of routine and worry, of where the next meal is coming from, of where to find shelter, of concern for how many degrees below the night might fall.

The gin helps me. Me, who never would have touched a drop. When I'm flush for a bottle, I find a quiet place and the gin takes me like a full moon shining between storm clouds on a dark night—I call these failings my little holidays. Yet, sometimes on a summer's day, as I sit on my bench by the old Flat Iron Building and the sun warms me, I watch the pigeons and pat the dogs as people walk them by, and I marvel at how, for a few short hours, life can be so extraordinarily wonderful.

The Library Card

Once you receive your Senior Citizen's Card you soon catch on to the necessary survival skills. For example, when attending matinee concerts at venues like Roy Thomson Hall or Hamilton Place, adopting a bent over slouch and shuffling your feet, invariably results in a nice young lady ushering you to your seat. Once, feigning an extra measure of instability, I was escorted by two nice young ladies. I do not have the indelicacy to pursue the technique to its logical conclusion, but who could blame an old guy for grabbing onto absolutely anything if he felt himself falling.

But it wasn't until I became a resident of Sunset Acres Home for the Aged, where its residents teach and practice survival skills every day, that I really understood the incredible power of senility.

I never had a better opportunity of practicing it than late one Saturday afternoon when carting my usual shelf of books through the wicket at my downtown library. I ran into a lady librarian who looked as if she'd had a strip torn off her by her boss and was ready to take it out on a golden-oldie.

"What's this?" she snapped, looking at the signature on my library card.

"It's my name," I said.

"I can't read *that*," she said. "It's illegible. I shall need some identification."

I gave her my driver's license and my credit card.

"I see you're from St. James. I shall need your St. James's Library Card."

Apparently, I had to belong to my local library before I could join the downtown

Library, and since I didn't pay taxes to that particular municipality, it cost $25 a year. But I had already paid that, months ago. I felt a twinge of annoyance. But they tell us at Sunset Acres never to lose our cool.

There were three possible ploys I might use. The *Aggression* ploy might have worked. This is where I would shout at the top of my voice, "I've been coming to this library for 75 years and I've never in my born natural been treated like this!" Then I would have brought my fist down with a bang on the counter. Noise is an awesome weapon in libraries. Darby, at Sunset Acres, could have pulled this off. Even with his stoop, he is still a big guy, but I've never been much for aggression.

I might have used the *Total Submission* ploy. This is where I would have burst into uncontrollable sobs. Joan at the Acres can turn this on and off at the drop of a hat. She does it in the middle of the Saturday-night singsong, usually when she is standing next to somebody large enough to catch her when she slumps. This is a most effective ploy when used in public for gaining immediate sympathy and turning the tables on an opponent. But I have difficulty producing tears at the best of times, and while now there were people behind me, none of them looked reliably *slump-able*. Besides, I couldn't trust myself not to laugh.

The *Senility* ploy was the obvious choice. At Sunset Acres we have long suspected that the young find something odious about the old if they still have a complete complement of their senses. From then on, I played the part of a benign simpleton ravaged by senility.

I knew exactly where my St. James's Library Card was. I spent a moment or two rummaging through my wallet. "Ah!" I said with a look of triumph, handing it to her.

"Ummph," she said, looking down on me as if I were a small child. "This is your Price-Warehouse Card," and she handed it back.

I looked at it as though I could scarcely believe she could have made such a stupid mistake. I held it close to my nose. I held it at arm's length. I held it up to my nose again. From a distance it might have looked as if I were playing a trombone.

"It's your Price-Warehouse Card," she reiterated. But I noticed the edge had gone off her voice. A number of people were now crowding behind me all taking an interest and she must have realized that to be rude to an old person in front of witnesses was tantamount to occupational suicide. I held up another card right in front of her eyes and she reared back.

"This is your Canadian Tire Card." I sensed a note of despair in her voice.

I took back the card. "Oh, I'm sooorry," I said. "Of course, it's my St. James's Library Card you want, isn't it?" I was nothing if not polite. At the Acres, I didn't get an *A+ in Sickening Ingratiation* for nothing. I held my wallet up to my nose and peered closely at the remaining cards. I took off my glasses, then carefully I put them in a case I had taken from my inside pocket, replacing them with another pair of identical prescription that I had taken from my other inside pocket. I could see from her expression, the ploy had given her faint hope. But not for long. I handed her my Bell Calling Card.

She gave a long sigh. I sensed the beginning of desperation. "Never mind, don't bother," she said, reaching out for one of my books.

But I had them all snug in a canvas bag that I had bought from the liquor store for a dollar. I wasn't having any of that. She wanted to see my St. James's Library Card and I was going to show it to her. I delved into my wallet again. I went through all my cards a couple of times, peering at them through my glasses and then raising my glasses and again holding them at arm's length. In turn I proffered her my Tottenham Library Card, my Senior's Card, my Canadian Citizenship Card and my Daguerreian Society Card, and somehow I managed to show her my Canadian Tire Card twice. One or two people behind me tried to help but we are warned at Sunset Acres always to keep up a front of staunch independence. I made sure they never got a good enough look at any of the cards to make a positive identification.

As a change of pace, at this point, I pulled the old *everything was too much for me* trick. This is a ploy based on the fact that disorganization is more contagious than the common cold. I fumbled and scattered my cards all over the floor. The people behind me were very kind and rushed to help me pick them up, for now there was quite a crowd. And as I stood there with my bag of books over one arm, my walking stick over the other, my wallet in one hand and a stack of cards, now in total disorder, in the other, I felt a welling of support. I had not experienced anything quite like this since, as a very small boy, I had been thrown into a pool wearing much too large water wings. The people behind were all rooting for me. So great was their support that I felt sure I could have pulled off the Sunset-Acres-Joan slumping ploy with one hundred percent certainty that somebody would have caught me. But that was unnecessary.

"It's here! It's here! I've found it!" I said, and the librarian tried to grab at it but I held it up and waved it at the people crowded behind. There was a spontaneous round of applause from those who now began to think they might get out before the library closed. I gave everybody a sheepish grin, for I felt a touch of feigned embarrassment was appropriate, and I handed the card to the library lady.

It was my Toys R'Them Card.

I had made my point. Slyly, by accident on purpose, I dropped the real St. James's Library Card on the floor. A lady behind me, to everyone's relief, picked it up and gave it to the librarian.

"Oh!" I said. "Is that it? I knew I had it somewhere, but you know how it is when you just can't put your finger on it."

The woman behind me gave a sympathetic nod.

I let the librarian process my books. By now they had opened up two more wickets to handle the milling crowd, but as I walked out through the thing that looks like a rose arbour and buzzes if you try to sneak out a book, I leaned back. "Sorry to be such a bother, but I have my St. Michael's Library Card too if you'd like to see it."

"Oh no! No! That won't be necessary," she said, visibly shrinking.

Sunset Acres would have been proud of me.

The Small Space beneath the Ceiling

It turned out to be a project over many years that started accidentally. She had reached the age when it was difficult to get down on her knees and even more difficult to get up again. So when several sheets of the newspaper fell to the floor, momentarily, she left them right where they fell. But one moment became another, and another. For several hours after, she fought the temptation to pick them up and the untidiness bothered her for several days. But for someone who had been so pernickety all her life, she was surprised how quickly she got used to it. So when, a day or two later, all of the newspaper dropped to the floor, she had less difficulty in leaving it right where it fell.

Her activities moved from the accidental to the accident-on-purpose stage. She would artfully nudge the *A & E* section off the table with her elbow. Sometimes, when she had nudged an especially large section, perhaps the *Classifieds* or *Business,* she would utter the word "Damn!" in case God were looking and listening.

Then there came a stage where, for a while, she was uncommitted. Nevertheless the number of newspapers on the floor still gradually increased. Then, one afternoon, without hesitation, without fanfare, without reservation, she threw a complete issue of *The Spectator* onto the floor. It was a new found freedom. The shackles of societal expectation fell away. For the first time in her life she felt incredibly free.

The floor was now covered with newspapers. There was no necessity to vacuum any more. In fact, even had she been able to unearth the vacuum cleaner, vacuuming would have been impossible. Dusting too seemed pointless. For the first few months, if she had had visitors, which she never did, the newspapers could have been explained by her making up a story that she was preparing to redecorate. But after a year or two, the thickness of the newsprint underfoot would have defied any logical explanation. Yet there was a logical explanation. Once she had removed herself from the expectations of society, what would make laying down newspapers any more absurd than any one of a thousand other things she might have done? She no longer cared what anyone thought.

Little by little, day by day, month by month, year by year, its gradualness making it almost unnoticeable, the incoming tide of newspapers took over her house at first, reaching the level of the chesterfield and chair seats, then inexorably, over the years, submerging all of the furniture. The table and the table lamps had long disappeared and so had the dresser. Only the top of an extra tall floor lamp was visible as the top of the CN Tower might have been from an aircraft on a day of low clouds. Certain exceptions had to be made. An arc drawn on the hinges of the front door was kept clear in order that the front door would open, but only enough for her to squeeze through.

But the newspapers had taken over more than the house. At first, she had had difficulty turning away from the orderliness of life. Now a new urgency had imposed itself with an even greater authority. For now she would wait expectantly for the arrival of the paperboy. With difficulty, she would wait until he'd gone before rushing to pick up the papers from the front porch. On the occasional day when he was sick, or on a holiday when there was no newspaper, she would suffer the agonies of withdrawal. In the beginning, she would read the papers first, but now her glasses were several years beneath her, eight inches or so above the table where she had inadvertently left them after reading *Regular Brake Care Pays Off* in the *Wheels* section. There was no time now to read them. In desperation she would tear the sections apart, laying down the sheets and filling the low spots. It would never have occurred to her that complete freedom was tyranny.

More exceptions had to be made. All sinks had long ago been buried but she could not do without the toilet and so the newspapers had been cleverly built around it. A detailed description would be superfluous.

A means of ascending to the top of the gradually filling rooms, a means by which she could climb to the very top layer where she lived, required a degree of ingenuity. Although a retired school teacher and well skilled in the techniques of *papier mâché*, the idea of fabricating steps was far too much for one whose major concern was not for creating, but for accumulating. So, almost by instinct, she engineered a ramp, which despite her total disregard for the creative, became, although she did not know it, a perfect logarithmic spiral—the curved equivalent of the golden mean.

While she imagined she did not care what people thought, this was not exactly the truth, for she was aware that her new style of living might be considered by some to be a form of madness. This was the case with others when their idea of her well-being was more important to them than her idea well-being, and so she kept the drapes closed and was careful to open the door only when she could be sure that nobody was watching.

Daily, her mind was filled with fragments: *Hong Kong Magnate Sells... Rural Women Must Go Without...*

Beautiful Buenos Aires... How to Fake an Organization... Darwin Beats God in Red America... Living in the Lap of Lechery... Sperm Donor Contest Touted for TV... Be a Helmet Head... Agent Dishes Dirt on Divas.... The short clipped headlines entered her head as by osmosis and just as quickly left again, for without her glasses, she could read only the large type.

It was in this new wonder that she lived, venturing out only for necessities. What began as an act of defiance had become a labour of love. It was a slow labour and in step with her life. Over the years she had considered ordering *The Expositor* in addition to *The Spectator*, and would have, had she not felt uncomfortable about changing the nature of her routine with regard to Time. There was something about the finiteness of one newspaper, but she was not so sure about two.

The accumulation continued until there was only the curvature of the ramp in the beauty of a rising nautilus, and a small space at the top into which she could barely squeeze, and where she slept. Her work was done, for when the quality of life approaches the unbearable, there is only one spur—to see what is about to happen next, and nothing would.

It was another accumulation of newspapers, this time between the door and the storm door—one that gradually expanded onto the porch as the paperboy continued to deliver them—that would bring her remarkable edifice to its inevitable conclusion.

One Late Payment

Alfred Smith was a man of impeccable honesty. He had lived life in the old style. Always paying his bills on time, paying off his mortgage, his car loans, all without as much as one late payment. It was not surprising that he had an AAA+ credit rating.

It was not surprising that he was continually bombarded with letters and phone calls encouraging him to apply for more credit cards. He shredded the letters and invariably cut the phone calls short.

He was approaching his eighty-sixth birthday when the idea came to him. He had always wanted to be a benefactor. He gave to charity whatever he could afford, but financial restraints precluded him from doing it on the grand scale that he would have liked. He had no heir, so in preparation for the inevitable, he had sold his house and car and everything else the previous year. Now he lived in a rented, furnished room on a very small pension. This was all that was required for his personal needs. He had put the monies from the disposal of his possessions to good charitable use. But he saw so much poverty, so much need, that it was heartbreaking for him to have to stand by, unable to do anything more about it.

Then he got the idea. The next time he received a letter inviting him to apply for a credit card, he did. The next time he received a phone call asking if his name might be put forward for the issue of a credit card, he said yes. Within two months he had acquired no less than seventeen credit cards and they kept on coming. He was surprised to find, that, in Canada alone, there were more than two hundred credit cards he could apply for.

When the local food bank needed a donation, he had a dozen cartons of baked beans delivered, charged to one of his cards. When the local drop-in center needed new furniture, he donated it and charged it to another of his credit cards. He began to have a reputation for getting things wholesale, so he was constantly buying this and that, charging it to his credit cards, and then selling it for whatever he could get for it, using the monies to pay the interest on the ever-mounting credit card debt. A midget hockey team got free uniforms. His was the largest donation to the Santa Claus Fund three years in a row. His donations to innumerable charities mounted, and so did his credit card debt.

He had little to do except crosswords, and it became a hobby juggling the cards, for he was very organized, using this to pay that, while gradually upping the limit on each card to accommodate the rising debt. Had there been anyone at the credit card companies who cared, they would have been delighted that someone of Alfred's impeccable reputation and AAA+ credit rating was doing business with them. The more the merrier, for that was how the system worked. Nobody bothered him as long as he kept paying the interest and Alfred never, never, never *ever* missed a payment.

One day the inevitable arrived. "I'd guess about six months," the doctor said, "give or take a month or two." Alfred wasn't fazed. He was approaching ninety. He simply changed up a gear or two, maximizing as many cards as he could and even taking out a few more, and still he never missed a payment. Yet, even if he had, and there had been someone at any of the 153 banks, credit card companies and store credit departments who cared, it is doubtful that they would have been unduly concerned, for that's the way the system worked and they knew that Alfred Smith had never missed a payment in his life.

"You should get your affairs in order," his doctor said on his last visit. The next day, Alfred took a cab to his bank and withdrew all his monies. He went home, packed it all in a cardboard box, some four hundred thousand dollars in one hundred dollar bills, for he had maximized the cash aspects of his credit cards too, and mailed it to the Salvation Army with a note that said, "Use for the poor and needy." He made sure the donation was anonymous so that it couldn't be traced later.

His doctor had given him good advice. Two weeks later an obituary appeared in the local paper. "Alfred Smith passed away peacefully at the Golden Gate Hospice. He supported numerous charities and was renowned for his generosity. His overwhelming concern for the poor and dispossessed was legendary." It ended with the prophetic phrase, "Alfred will be greatly missed."

The Dog, Parish

What made it difficult for Eyton Slep to determine if it was in his head, or if it was really in amongst the hawthorns at the bottom of the garden was that the people in the village lived as much inside their heads as in the village itself.

If he had been an artist and you had asked him to sketch Chipping Whimsdon, he would have sketched it much as it was when he first came some seventy years ago. Only occasionally had it been necessary for him to update his mental image. When they chopped down the huge willow tree in Mrs. Hamstall's garden, for instance, or after the war, when the main street was rerouted to the left of the memorial.

Newcomers lived in a different village, the village of brick, stone and macadam—the village that could be plotted on an Ordinance Survey Map. But they were not privy to the village that was discussed in the Red Lion, or in the church hall, or in the post office, or in the library, or in Leona Fenny's store. This was the village to which Neddy Bream, the gravedigger, belonged, yet he had been dead these forty years. This was the village in which the scandal of Fred Brockleton's bicycle left outside Etti Martin's cottage all one night was as vivid today as it was fifteen years ago. For the true villagers, Chipping Whimsdon was an encyclopedia of memories to which its inhabitants unwittingly owed their identities. Eyton Slep was a part of this legend and although it raised a few eyebrows when it slipped out that he had once edited the atheist gazette, *God Not*, he was regarded as one of the more level-headed seniors in the community.

"It" was what he called it, for he didn't know what it was and there was not a single noun that seemed adequate. He noticed it for the first time the previous spring. Having finished the Sunday crossword, he went down the garden to prune the raspberry canes and caught sight of it out of the corner of his eye. He swung his head quickly to look where he thought it should be, amongst the hawthorn bushes, but when his vision cleared, there was nothing. The experience considerably unnerved him.

Always it was like that. He would see it only out of the corner of his eye. When he would turn his head to look, it was as though he had been staring into a bright light and looked away. There were blind spots in his visual field, which, having cleared in a second or two, revealed nothing.

A week or two after it first appeared he saw it again in the same place, but this time his dog, Parish, was with him. When he turned to look, Parish was staring into the hawthorn bushes, crouched, growling softly and obviously terrified. He backed cautiously away and then turned and ran through a hole in the fence towards the escarpment. The dog had been his companion for more than ten years but Eyton never saw him again. Nor did anyone else, apparently, for a notice on the lost-and-found board in the hardware store and on the slate in the Red Lion brought not a single clue.

He could not describe it, though it always had the same characteristics: animal, dwarf-like, with glittering eyes, and always it came out of darkness. Eyton was frightened. He knew, beyond doubt, it was malevolent. He avoided that part of the garden, letting the raspberries go to frost that year, and he put thick drapes over the kitchen window, for he would sometimes catch sight of it out of the corner of his eye while he was preparing his meals. It worried him constantly, for he knew it was there even when he could not see it. Then on a winter's evening, when he was returning from the Red Lion, he saw it again. This time it was not amongst the hawthorns but in the alley between Riche's seed barn and the dilapidated building that used to be the old smithy. He did not attempt to look more closely, there was no point, but pulling his overcoat around him he hurried home. After that he began to see it everywhere. It came out of dark shadows, under a culvert, in a shady thicket, out of the umbra under a farm cart. This dwarfed and hunched animal with piercing eyes manifestly evil was always watching and waiting for him.

Now he moved with an obvious uncertainty looking furtively about him. He became the frequent subject of conversation over a pint in the Red Lion. One or two of his friends tried to talk to him, but whatever it was, he was not about to share it with them, for he feared they would think he was going mad. One evening in the pub, thinking it was watching him from a far corner, he swung round with such quickness that he knocked a tray of drinks out of Elsie Maynard's hands. "Look what you're doing, you old fool!" she yelled. Afterwards she apologized, but he was so mortified he never went into the Red Lion again.

It appeared to the villagers that he became more and more eccentric. Soon he was a recluse, draping his living room windows with heavy curtains too, and putting a lamp in every corner of every room. Jed Mullins at the hardware, claimed he used five gallons of lamp oil a month.

The village presumed that it was senile dementia, but even it was surprised when he insisted that he was a murderer. Constable Blewitt sent in a report to his sergeant in Dorchester. But Eyton had already ridden his bike down to the Dorchester police station and pleaded to be put in a cell. Sergeant Carns had sent him on his way. "Just you get along home, old fellow," he had said. "We'll investigate it." But investigate what?—the alleged strangling of an unnamed woman almost sixty years ago, no record of a missing person, twelve-thousand acres of bog to search for the body, and the suspect's police record—convicted of having no rear light on his bicycle? As a formality, Sergeant Carns sent Constable Blewitt out to look around Dimtry Fen, but as expected, his report was inconclusive.

Gresham Fields shared a new vicar with the village. Eyton came to him in the vestry one morning. But his story was so garbled, so intertwined with pleas for forgiveness and snatches of New Testament prayers, his presence so obviously paranoid, that the reverend came to the same conclusion as Sergeant Carns—that he had gone a little soft in the head. "Come to the service on Sunday and we will talk more about it," he had said. But he hoped that Eyton would just go away. And Eyton did.

Beth Leath cleaned for him and it was fortunate that she was there the morning he collapsed in the garden. His neighbour, Dan Gurney, helped put him to bed and they sent for Doc Chalmers. "No point in moving him to the cottage hospital," the Doc said. "He won't last the day." So they sent for Jenny, his neighbour. The first stroke took his speech and as darkness fell, he made frantic gurgling noises until they lit every lamp. His eyes worked frantically from left to right, but still he struggled for life.

On the third day, a second stroke paralyzed his left side, but still his eyes moved as though he were looking for something, yet afraid that he would see it, and still he would not die. On the fifth day, Jeremiah Bewd, an old friend, came to see him. "Let go, Eyton," he said. "It ain't for us old uns to hang on like this. Why don't you let go?" But Eyton fixed him with a terrified stare and when it was time for him to leave, despite the paralysis, Jeremiah had to pry each of Eyton's fingers from around his wrist.

The room was fetid from the smoke of the oil lamps, and once Beth tried to open the drapes to let in some air, but he became frenzied and she was forced to close them again. Around six on the evening of the seventh day, although the fire was well stoked, a chill came upon the room, and with a terrible howl he surrendered the remnants of his strength and was drawn, struggling, into the vortex.

Beth and Jenny washed him, laid him out, tied up his jaw and placed the coins on his eyelids, but not by any manipulation could they relieve his expression of stark terror.

A group of villagers that night congregated in Eyton's kitchen over fresh-brewed tea, fortified with brandy that Jenny found on a shelf over the stove. "Never seen one like that in all my born natural. The old uns are usually glad to go," said Ed Minton. "Guess it was the dementia. It gets em like that sometime." And the gathering cheered to anecdotes woven through the years of Eyton's life. And as the warmth from the stove, the brandy, and the conversation mellowed the gathering, there was a sudden scratching at the door.

"I'll get it," said Beth, rising and opening the door. "Well! If it ain't Parish. Eyton's dog's come back."

Little Black Book

I'm not by any means an unbeliever, just somebody who has neglected his spiritual side a little bit. But then, I don't take my car in for service frequently enough either. So when I saw this twosome, each carrying a copy of the Good Book, coming towards me across the bowling greens—I was going to spread fertiliser at the time—I had the suspicion I was about to be saved, and my heart sank. Not because I had been singled out to be saved—I was flattered at the thought—but because I suspected that the attempt would be made with the utmost pedestrian monotony.

Four decades of television commercials, bringing with them the modern necessity for assimilating two hundred and fifty images a minute, had developed my mind, for better or worse, to where it could no longer be stimulated by reluctant discussions on *ad hoc* selections from the Scriptures, out of context. In fact, the two hundred and fifty images couldn't do that either.

I also suspected I was going to be part of a ritual and I would ultimately count as a statistic and find myself numbered in a small book as part of the day's "take" so to speak. It reminded me of when I was a small boy and used to collect railway locomotive numbers. But I can never be outright rude to people, so I figured that instead of the fascination of fertiliser-spreading, I was in for twenty minutes of unmitigated boredom.

The conversation opened with the usual trite banalities, which didn't surprise me since, in an earlier day and for a short time, I had been a Fuller Brush salesman myself. They were extremely polite and pleasant young fellows, but it wasn't long before the tall one was into *Revelation 17:5*, with a vengeance. He put his narrative together like a computer programmed not to leave spaces between the words, but this didn't faze me. "I wonder if you fellows could answer a question about the parables for me," I interrupted. The tall one stopped in his tracks. The short one's mouth fell open. Obviously, they had never been confronted by this situation before. "I'm puzzled by the *Parable of the Tares*," I said. "Is a tare a particular kind of weed or is it a term used to denote the overall genre?" Before they could answer I'd led them on to the greens and pointed out two or three different weed species. Now, there's not much you need to know about weeds unless it's how to get rid of them. But over the years I had picked up a fair few facts about them—things like "picking dandelions makes you wet the bed" kind of stuff. Before I realised it, I had given them a good ten minutes of my weed-trivia.

Considering how much the Old Testament depends on vegetable metaphors I was surprised how little they knew about weeds!

But by now, the tall one was back into the Scriptures. This time it was Nehemiah. "Funny you should bring him up," I interrupted again. "He is the only biblical character who has ever had a fungus named after him." And I led them over to green number eight where there were still the remnants of snow-mould. "See that," I said, "it's *Fusarium nivale,* a very similar fungus to *Nehemiah nivale,*" and I got them down on their knees to look at the spores. Fortunately, I had on my old pants, for I hadn't noticed the greens were still wet. But I was able to show them examples of *Typhula, Marasmius oreades* and *Sclerotinia homoeocarpa*. At the end of twenty minutes I'd wager those two fellows could name and identify all the moulds, commonly affecting bent grass.

By now I had got the short one pushing the fertiliser spreader. The tall one kept apologising for taking up so much of my valuable time. "Don't concern yourself in the least," I said. "I've got an hour—two hours if necessary. One of the joys of retirement is you can afford the occasional extravagance of time. And besides, it's a real pleasure talking to you," I said. I'd never run into anybody before who could make the Scriptures sound so interesting. And by the time we had walked back to the clubhouse I had explained to them the advantages of using chlorothalonil over mancozeb in controlling algae, and since I walk real slow these days, I had time to give them a short course on how to eliminate moss using several applications of copper sulphate.

The last I saw of them they were walking almost at a dogtrot up West Street. Curiously they didn't knock on any more doors. I do believe the tall one was staggering slightly, perhaps not feeling too well; I had noticed earlier, his eyes were glazed. "Don't you forget now," I shouted, as they reached the High Street, "never water late into the evening!" The short one turned and waved weakly.

You know, I never did ask what denomination they were; we just got so engrossed with those Scriptures there was never an opportunity. But I did feel terribly guilty after they'd gone. After all, I had misjudged them. It goes to show you can never go by first appearances, can you? I didn't find either of them the least bit boring. And who would have thought that those two nice young men would have had such an extraordinary interest in grass?

I wonder if they made a note of me in their little book!

Camera Obscura

I

Hormones, a falling out with her family, a hot and humid summer night, and a full moon over Brightly's levee contrived for young Elsie Smith a world in which, for the first time in her life, she outdistanced her loneliness and embraced her deliverance with such abandon there was not an instant for a thought of the consequence.

She left home before the baby was born, naming it Stephen Norri after its profligate father Latham Norri, soon abbreviated to S. Norri, and then to Snorri... Smith.

His mother went on to become a good-time girl with an infallible taste for worthless men, and in the wake of the inevitable breakdown of her relationships, an aftertaste for moving on to the next town.

Snorri tagged along in the detritus of near poverty, avoiding the infection and contagion of communal thought so that he never became part of the great collective unconscious that, for most of us, provides the feelings of time and place in which we surround ourselves with walls of comfort.

Had he stayed in one place long enough to make friends, they would have told you that Snorri Smith was intelligent. Most of us, realizing one place is much the same as another, stay put. Snorri, for that very reason, moved on. In a procession of small towns, he spent much of his time in libraries and so had a profound knowledge of many subjects.

He could tell you the angles of the facets for a gem of the marquise cut, or how many cars per hour a given highway could carry without overloading. He could relate the experiments leading up to the proof of Boyle's law, and subjects as diverse as astronomy and sub-atomic particle theory were well within his capacity for discourse if ever he had occasion. His knowledge of literature was equally complete and he would have been unbeatable on any of the television quiz shows. Yet, Snorri did absolutely nothing with his knowledge and since he avoided anyone with whom he might have had discussion, its acquisition was merely the means of spending the time of his life.

He was a man of few words who was dedicated to maintaining a remote equilibrium. He did this by never allowing his rare causes for celebration to become the seeds of ambition, or allowing his disappointments to undermine his morale.

Yet, despite his eccentricity, he was careful always to present an image of respectability. He was decently dressed and physically there was nothing about him that was particularly noticeable. He tended to merge into the commonplace. His background, should he be investigated, would turn up nothing out of the ordinary. He had learned early that his innocence would be compromised by the stigma of *no fixed address*. So he had a Post Office Box number and a house number and street in a remote part of a remote state that with the name "Smith" would be difficult to corroborate. As much as possible, he insulated himself from society.

But there was one inevitable contact. He needed a means of visible, or better still invisible support, and though he took only that which he needed for his frugal existence, the police would have termed him a B&E boy, a cat burglar, since he invariably made his entrance through an upper floor window. Over the years he'd had several lucky escapes, but so far had never been caught. This was not surprising since he was extraordinarily cautious. Unlike many of his kind, he had never become overconfident. He never approached his crimes in haste or lightly. He planned his footloose wanderings carefully. He kept a comfortable sum in a remote bank account so that he was rarely desperate for money and could always plan and case his next job in a leisurely fashion. His profession was one of convenience, but had there been an honest means of making his living that was of equal stealth, he might well have taken it, for he was not lazy, or greedy, or angry at society.

Some weeks previous he had broken into an old warehouse and picking the lock on a cupboard he had found gold wire. There were two coils; one appeared to be in daily use. The other, perhaps in reserve, was still wrapped. He took only the wrapped coil, and re-locking the cupboard, left the premises, leaving no evidence. It could be days or weeks before the Company realized the wire was missing and they might never know there had been a break in. By then, he would be three or four towns away.

The 4 p.m. Greyhound had just pulled into the bus station. The priority was to find a motel. He preferred motels to renting a room; they were less personal. He found a place on top of the hill that, like several of the older and cheaper motels, had been bypassed by the new highway. He never unpacked. Travelling light, he carried a small valise containing a change of clothing, his toiletries, and a manuscript. If he had to account for where he was and why, he would claim he was an author writing a book on the architecture of small towns.

Among his few possessions was a camera, a flashlight and a single piece of thin steel wire, which might have come adrift from the hinge of the valise.

The proceeds from the coil of gold wire would not last forever and the next morning he scouted the town.

There are two kinds of people: those who overtly secure their valuables with grills, bars and alarms; and those who trust in the dubious security of their valuables remaining inconspicuous. It was the latter who usually found themselves to be Snorri Smith's victims.

He made his way to the town's industrial area and under the guise of taking photographs, methodically gauged the potential of several buildings. One in particular struck him as having possibilities. It was a gaunt old stone building of four stories standing alone in the middle of an otherwise vacant lot, all of the adjacent buildings having been demolished. A disused railway siding ran along one side. It had probably been an old factory years ago, but he had found many similar buildings contained rented offices or workshops, which often harboured small items of considerable value. He had a nose for such places and had done well out of them. The security of this place looked overdone for its unprepossessing appearance. There was a solitary sign carved in stone over the portal. *Optical Antiquities* was all it read. On the east side was a third-floor window, which could be reached with moderate difficulty from a sloping tin roof and a conduit that ran up the wall adjacent to it. The approach was inconspicuous. This would be it, he thought, and retracing his steps to the centre of the town, spent the rest of the day in its library.

At five-thirty, he walked around the corner to a Bar and Grill, had a substantial meal, then returning to the motel, he waited till dusk.

Taking all his belongings, so that in case of trouble he could hide out through the night and take the first bus out in the morning, he made his way back to the industrial district. By now it was almost dark and any employees from the neighbouring factories had left for the day. Hiding his valise under a pile of debris, he took with him his flashlight and the piece of wire in case he needed to pick a lock. He scorned the use of jimmies, preferring skill to brute force.

Taking up a vantage some distance from the building he stood and watched for several minutes. There was no sign of activity. He walked quickly across the lot. With a single leap he was on the corrugated roof and within seconds reached the level of the third-floor window. It was not wired, and to his surprise, it opened easily, sliding to the right; he would not have to remove his glove to use the diamond in the ring on his index finger to cut the glass. Heaving himself up onto the sill, which was solid stone and all of two and a half feet thick, he disappeared inside.

He found himself in an iron duct, which he presumed was part of the heating system. A weight on a sash-cord and pulley closed the window behind him automatically. Curious, but all to the good, he thought; nothing was more suspicious to a prowling police officer than the sight of an open window.

He began to crawl along the duct when, without warning, it tilted and he was helpless to prevent himself sliding headlong. At the end of the duct he fell several more feet onto a hard surface.

Dazed but otherwise unhurt, he took a minute or two to gather his wits in the darkness.

His first inclination was to think he might have stumbled into a processing plant, perhaps an old brewery, for the floor on which he was lying was concave and felt like the interior of a tank. Luckily, he had the presence of mind to hang on to the flashlight though it was no longer working.

Once, he had been lost in the pitch-black of a factory with a burned out flashlight, and not daring to switch on a light, it had taken him most of the night to find his way out. Since then he had carried a spare bulb.

Changing the bulb, he was almost afraid of what he might see. The dim spider web of light revealed the inside of an iron culvert. From the appearance of the rust and the rivets it was likely an old steam boiler about four metres long and a little more than three metres in diameter.

Little by little he pieced together what must have happened. The duct leading from the window by which he had entered was pivoted like a teeter-totter. As he had crawled over its fulcrum it had tilted until he had slid off its end, then it returned to its horizontal position. A piece of iron welded to its underside now completely blocked the aperture from which he had entered.

Like a man who cannot credit the loss of his wallet to a pickpocket, and persists in thinking it has been mislaid through his own carelessness, and that if he will keep on looking, he will eventually find it and the problem will resolve itself, Snorri Smith held desperately to the hope that his predicament was the result of sheer accident. But already, in the deepest recesses of his mind was the suspicion that he was the victim of a contrivance of an ominous malevolence.

The flashlight beam revealed little more on subsequent scans than it did on the first, revealing only an iron container for which there was apparently no entrance or exit. He was imprisoned in a rusting iron cylinder. The air, if not fresh, was breathable and the temperature was about that of the outside. Painfully, he stood up with the intention of examining the further end of his prison, but as he walked forward this cylinder also began to tilt and he stepped back hastily. Another teeter-totter, he thought, but why? The tilt was not sudden but slow as the shift of his weight over the fulcrum overcame the residual weight of the tank, or so he thought. Little by little, he built up his courage until he could slowly rock the tank, like children rock a seesaw, by standing straddled across its centre. By patient and careful trial he determined that he could rock the cylinder only until it reached a slope of about forty degrees where a stop prevented it tilting further.

It was then he noticed by the dim flashlight that as his prison tilted, a moon-shaped gap opened up at the lower end, which was large enough for him to have slipped through had he not been standing. Further investigation suggested that the tank tilted independent of the end-plate. This was left vertical leaving an aperture at the base of the sloping end of the tank. He tried to see where the gap led to but the flashlight revealed nothing. He began to wonder if the pit were bottomless, for there was no sound from a nickel flipped into it.

Imagine if you can, a straight-sided tumbler laid on its side and teetering on a fulcrum. Standing vertically across the open end, is a piece of card. When the open end of the tumbler is pushed down, independent of the piece of card, it leaves a half-moon shaped aperture between the bottom of the tumbler and the lower edge of the card, through which anything in the sloping glass might slide. This was precisely the construct in which he found himself.

It was then that he noticed the two troughs above the gap, fixed to the vertical and immovable end-plate. One was filled with water, though he was not thirsty. The other was filled with a light coloured powder. Later he would discover that each time the tank tilted and returned to the horizontal, the troughs would be replenished. He would also find the powder was a form of edible cereal.

All of these revelations took place in the first few hours. He fought to keep down a sense of panic. Even now he had not fully realized his awful predicament. Wearily, he clawed his way back up the tilted tank until his weight returned it to its horizontal position.

His understanding drained him of all energy. He was left with only the doubtful consolation that tomorrow there might be people about and he would attract their attention. That he was there unlawfully and that he might be arrested was already of little consequence to him. But as he peered into the opaque darkness, his last thought before falling into an exhausted sleep was: *How will I know when it is tomorrow?*

Tomorrow came in the terror of his waking.

The events of the previous night, left to the mastication of his subconscious, woke him in the horror of his circumstance. Involuntarily he began to scream; so great was his terror that at first he could not form words. He screamed until he was exhausted like a child that cries itself out, then as he regained strength, he screamed again, each renewed sequence less fanatical than the last, until after several hours he was reduced to a pathetic whimpering.

So well insulated was his cell that the vowels and syllables of his speech, and even his screams, died in his throat and the tapping of his flashlight upon the bare metal of the tank sounded but a grudging knell starved of resonance.

He was a prisoner of sound too, for no sound was to reach him from outside, and as time progressed he would crave the peal of church bells carrying across the countryside, for sound is part of the essence of humanity.

But the mind out of control does not govern the body for long. His outbursts had given him a thirst, and moving cautiously to the centre of the tank he eased his weight on to the further end until it tilted. With his hands held out before him he took hesitant steps down the sloping floor until he felt its rigid end-plate. Feeling for the trough, he cupped the water into the palm of his hand and drank.

His emotional outbursts had dulled the edge of his fear and taking hold of himself he resolved to fully investigate the interior. The tank had been rusting for years but it was still sturdy. An iron plate three quarters of the way up the boiler's side now covered the aperture through which he had fallen; it could not be moved. The only way out was through the gap that appeared when the tank was tilted. Again he shifted his weight and, tilting the tank, walked awkwardly, with his feet widely spaced, down to its lower end. By lying dangerously on his stomach, headfirst down the precarious slope while gripping the end of the tank, he could look over the edge, but pointing his flashlight down he saw nothing but blackness. Dropping his last dime merely confirmed the pit was bottomless for there was no sound.

Taking stock of the situation he concluded that he was not in immediate danger. His weight would keep the tank horizontal and if he was careful when manipulating the tilt of the tank in his moves for food and water, there was little chance he would fall into the void that opened when the tank was tilted. As long as the food and water held out he might live for months, possibly years. Sometimes he took solace from this. Sometimes the thought terrified him.

That night he ate his first meal. The powdered cereal was bland but edible. He found it could be mixed with water to make a kind of cold porridge.

He went through his pockets. His wallet held several small bills, and in the interest of his subterfuge, a photograph of somebody else's wife and children. There was the piece of thin wire, a half-finished packet of breath mints, several tissues and a comb. On his wrist was a utilitarian Timex without a luminous dial, and on his finger the diamond ring. His clothes consisted of: vest, underpants, shirt, jeans, a padded jacket, gloves, a toque, socks and black running shoes. He also found a book of matches with three remaining.

Each time he would tilt the tank, which was at least once a day, when he needed food and water, anything carelessly left on its floor would slide or roll into the void. In the darkness it was going to require extraordinary care to make sure that all his possessions were safely secured in his pockets if they were not to be lost.

It occurred to him that he would only be able to tell the time for as long as the flashlight batteries lasted.

The edge of fear is honed by the immediacy of danger, and now terror had temporally receded beyond the threshold of a persistent anxiety that could only be alleviated by exhaustion. The blackness fell upon him like laudanum.

He had continued to examine the tank until the batteries of the flashlight gave out, and using his last three matches, he had dropped the lighted tissues into the void but still he saw nothing.

Anonymous days and weeks coalesced in the generic dark.

In the beginning he played mind games, wrote poetry in his head and for a while the fertility of his imagination, fuelled by his store of knowledge, was a match for the deadly monotony, but not for long. His routine soon became the timetable of his bodily needs; when he was hungry he ate, when he was thirsty he drank, when he was tired he slept. Perception is the register of change, and memory its measure; the deadly similarity of his hours soon fell below the threshold of the sensitivity of either. The monotony of the present did not stimulate his perceptions, nor was its sameness committed to memory, until time stopped and the natural activity of his brain slowed just short of coma.

Then the hallucinations began.

In his lucid moments he was terrified that in his delusions he would slip into the void, for in his disorientation he could no longer distinguish fantasy from reality. He was transported to worlds of unspeakable horror where the prospect of death was merciful. Yet sometimes, there were more subtle delusions in which he would experience falling through the void onto a feather mattress, then in his delirium, he would rise and walk through an open door into summer sunlight. In the remnants of his sanity he knew better than to expect so benevolent a deliverance.

The near-vacuum of his mind held only questions. What was the purpose of this place? Why was he here? Where was God in this tank? What was the motive behind a mind that had contrived such inhumanity? The answers to such puzzles were not to be found in the juxtaposition of the pieces of his past knowledge, nor in the immediate or future fabrications of his imagination. The illogic of his circumstance could only be ameliorated by faith, and faith was a cloud with a silver lining. He could not accept that he was the victim of impersonal misfortune. He could not bear the thought that his situation lacked a reasonable explanation.

Perhaps he was part of a grotesque experiment. There was a comfort in the belief that he might be watched and, from time to time, he would voice a plea for forgiveness of the unknown malignancy, and he realized that he was praying.

At first, he was scrupulously careful of his possessions, but the darkness and the silence had dulled his vigilance. His flashlight and comb were gone. In the sly and gradual demolition of passing time he was reduced to a callous poverty of body, mind and spirit. It was then that he saw the light.

At first he thought it was his imagination; darkness plays tricks upon the retina. But moving his head back, there it was again: less than a pinpoint of light at the top of the farthest end of the tank. There was light entering through so small a hole that he could see it only when his eye was directly in line. Holding his hand stationary, palm outwards, he moved his head until he could see an image on his palm. It was a faint image of the sun. He was wildly excited.

He stood up, taking care to keep the image in the centre of his palm; he was terrified that if he lost track of it he would never find it again. Edging forward, he tilted the tank and precariously shuffled his way to the lower end. As he did so, the image on his palm seemed to increase slightly in intensity as he brought his raised hand within inches of the boiler-plate. The image remained on the palm of his hand for some minutes before it gradually disappeared.

The hole in the end boilerplate was acting like a pinhole in a pinhole camera. Smith realised there must have been a window outside that end of the tank and had the hole been of reasonable diameter, everything outside would have been imaged on the inside. But the hole was so small that only an object the brightness of the sun could be observed, and then for only a few minutes until the thickness of the iron plate vignetted the image.

This pathetic stimulus, for the first time in an eternity of darkness, had lifted the torpor from his mind and when hunger signified that it was time for his next meal he added the fragments of his last breath mint as flavour. He was conscious of a sublime happiness before he drifted into profound and peaceful sleep.

When he awoke his mind was overflowing with thoughts of his discovery of the pinhole. Quickly he moved into the approximate position from where he had seen it previously. He would move his head, raise it slightly, move it back and forth, lower his head slightly, move it back and forth, peering intently into the dark until his complete attention was focused on this single activity. It was with agitation that he would attend to his ablutions for fear he might miss the narrow window of light. There was no certainty that it would appear again; the day might be overcast or perhaps, like prehistoric stone circles or the pyramids, the diameter of the hole might be sufficient only to project the sun for a few minutes each year, depending upon its azimuth.

Then, after what seemed an eternity, it appeared and he found himself laughing like a demented idiot.

This time, capturing the sun's image on his palm, he traced it back to where it would naturally project onto the tank wall. Lying on his stomach and taking a close look, he took the short length of steel wire from his pocket and marked a point where the image fell. As it moved, the dots he scribed formed a shallow arc until as the sun moved out of alignment with the hole, again the image disappeared.

He could no longer tell if his sleeping punctuated days, but the image would now appear at regular intervals which he guessed were every twenty-four hours, and his expectation of their appearance now became of intense concern and the very focus and purpose of his life. He would wait patiently, moving his head from side to side, and when he detected the pinhole he would be filled with elation. After several sightings, and as he continued to plot the traverse of the image across the end of the tank, he noticed there was a previously inscribed geometric pattern parallel and similar to his own.

Someone must have traced this same pattern, but who, and when?

The image of the sun was less than the diameter of a dime and very faint. He could see only the area of the tank wall covered by its image. From his inscription he could tell that, each day, the track moved slightly higher than the day previously, and since the image within the tank was an inversion of the world outside, it indicated that the sun was slightly lower in the sky. He knew from this that the earth had passed the summer solstice and that the days were becoming shorter. The traverse of the sun's image followed a downward curve and he knew the sun must be rising and that it was before noon.

Each of these discoveries gave him the most exquisite thrill and he felt once again that he was a possession of the world.

The image would not appear for very long, for as the sun's path became lower in the sky, its alignment would cause the light passing through the pinhole to be baffled by the thickness of the boiler-plate until it was no longer visible. He would not see it again until the following year when the sun would be in the same quadrant.

He plotted the course of the sun for ten to twelve days with one or two gaps, which he attributed to cloud cover. But on the last day he was to receive a bonus. As he peered intently at the moving image of the sun, letters appeared scribed into the rusting metal. As each was illuminated by the sun's image, he committed it to memory: J-A-S-O-N and then a small gap and W-I-L-D-E and then there was more, O-C-T-1-9-1-2.

Jason Wilde, Oct 1912.

If it was now really October then he must have been incarcerated for seven months.

Perhaps there were some aberrations in Wilde's calculations of eighty odd years before but if Wilde knew it was October when he wrote the date by the light of the pinhole image, unless the tank had been moved, he could not think of a reason why it should not be October now.

Eighty years, he pondered. *What happened to Wilde?*

The very contemplation sent him into a depression, and as the time indolently passed, and day by day it became evident that he had seen the last of the pinhole images, the depression deepened. He craved the sound of a human voice, and the cries of gulls. The smack and hiss of the surf along the sea wall that he remembered from childhood reduced him to pitiful sobbing. He was plagued by the remembrance of the taste of sharp cheddar, and as he sank deeper into the contrivances of his imagination, he feared he would go mad.

He was now scarcely recognisable as human.

At first he had attempted to keep himself clean, but the trough held limited water and could only be replenished by leveling and then tilting the tank. This had to be accomplished in pitch darkness on a forty-degree slope and while he kept a firm grip on his clothes. After losing the flashlight, which fell out of his pocket, and nearly losing his jacket, he decided washing was not worth the risk and after a while there seemed little purpose to it. His hair was long and matted, as was the struggle of his beard, and his clothes were ragged and stiff with filth.

These things were of little consequence compared to the ravages of his mind, for again the relentless darkness and the silence began to take their toll. But luckily the hallucinations did not return, for soon he would have more pressing concerns.

It was a very gradual change so at first he thought he must be imagining that it was easier to tilt the tank and more difficult to bring it back to the horizontal. Eventually he noticed that he was no longer able to lie full-length down the centre of the tank without it beginning to tilt.

Then a terrible realization struck him.

From the beginning he had somehow presumed that the tank would be horizontal when it was at rest and that it was his weight that caused it to tilt.

What a fool he had been. The tank was at rest when it was tilted forty degrees! It was his body weight that kept it horizontal. Cautiously, he moved to the far end of the tank, tilting it in the process. Placing his hands on each of the troughs he raised his weight off the floor. The tank did not move; it remained tilted.

He knew he was doomed.

He was like a child on the low end of a seesaw, on the other end of which there was a weight. The child could maintain its position on the ground only as long as it weighed more than the weight. If the child continued to take stones out of its pocket it would eventually be powerless to prevent the weight from raising its end of the seesaw.

Several times he had had to make new holes in his belt with the length of wire. He knew he had been losing weight and for some time after the pinhole affair he had lost the will to eat. The cereal was bland and unappetising and it was difficult to consume more than was necessary to quell the pangs of hunger. Besides, the powder might not have had sufficient nutritious value to maintain his weight, regardless. Either way, sooner or later, his fate was inevitable.

With this change of circumstance came a change in attitude, for he could not resist a grudging respect for an intelligence that could contrive so exquisite a machine. A machine that could trap and torture its victim, then evacuate itself, ready for its next sacrifice. All that was required was a hopper with a few hundred pounds of the nutrient; the water could be replenished from a rainwater tank on the roof, and the device could go on processing its victims for years, perhaps hundreds of years.

Its initiator could be ten thousand miles away or might even be dead.

Now he understood the poet's truth in "months that wound and the final month that kills", for he was, literally, Prufrock, measuring out his life by coffee spoons. The status quo once given now must be earned, and living would acquire a new urgency.

He began by stuffing himself, forcing himself to eat when he was not hungry. Sometimes he would fill up on water. For a while he succeeded in reversing the process and for a while he was able to sleep, as he used to, stretched out down the length of the tank. But though, temporarily, he might have gained weight, it was not enough that he needed to let out his belt, and gradually he began to notice, once again, he was losing ground to the demands of the tank.

Panic began to set in and he was beset by a relentless anxiety, which drove him to renewed determination. His life became one continuous demand to swallow more and more of the cold and tasteless gruel. In the beginning the hours dragged with the virus of a lassitude that paralysed the mind, but now signs of the deterioration of his stability came with such rapidity that it seemed to him that time was in free fall.

Though his desperate perseverance slowed the inevitable he realized that his potential for maintaining the tank in its horizontal position was diminishing. His presence became hostage to a singular necessity, which he pursued to the boundaries of exhaustion. All else was subservient. He lived the nightmare of a dream-like waking, interspersed with fragments of jagged sleep.

He could no longer sleep stretched out along the length of the tank. He had to lie in the foetal position. Still he stuffed himself with the flat flavourless food, nauseated at the very thought of it. But it did not stop his ever-gradual weight loss until the only way in which he could keep the tank from tilting was to lie crosswise pressed against its end so that his body weight gave maximum leverage.

Manoeuvring down the full-length of the sloping tank became even more dangerous. Fear that he might stop to think, kept him going. Again he ate and drank and splashed his clothes with water and daubed himself with the cereal and stuffed handfuls into his pockets and down the front of his shirt. Then, clambering up the slope, he levelled and tilted the tank again to replenish the water in the trough. Taking off his shoe, he filled it with more water and for a while, by this means, he was able to bulk up his weight sufficiently to level the tank. He was able to catch only snatches of sleep, before being awakened by the tank tilting again as the water seeped away or evaporated.

Several times he woke to find himself sliding or rolling out of control. Several times he miraculously grabbed his shoes and gained his feet, barely avoiding sliding through the gap. But inevitably, there came a time when, while he saved himself, he could not save his precious shoes which, filled with water, had provided several pounds of ballast.

He knew now that he no longer had the means to level the tank.

He was left leaning against the vertical end-wall, his feet on the edge of the floor. Under him was the void.

When the tank was dry he could lie on its sloping floor by hanging on to a weld seam with his fingertips and digging his feet in between the rivets, but it took effort and he could only do it for a few minutes. Now, he had lost his shoes and the floor of the tank was wet and slimy.

He was safe as long as he remained standing. He was safe as long as he did not fall asleep.

So desperate was his position that there was no longer time for contemplation. He was trapped on the surface of consciousness. All potential for ingenuity was gone. By turns he cursed and pleaded with the perverted mind of the architect of his fate. Sometimes he sang the songs of his boyhood. His head would jerk as he awoke petrified from an instant's sleep. Lustily he would sing again to stave off a despair that craved oblivion.

Without concept of time, he was unaware it was the afternoon of the fourth day after he had lost his shoes when he finally crumpled, and reaching feebly for the edges of the tank, slipped into the void.

II.

They found him under a front porch; a dog would not stop barking. He was mute. Nobody had any idea how he had gotten there. Emaciated, barefoot, he scarcely resembled a man. Nobody could fathom why he was covered in feathers.

They say he slept for several days.

Later, at the infirmary when he had been bathed and shaved, his appearance was that of a death camp survivor. His skin was drawn like a bat's wing and his eyes, as though bleached and enlarged, gave him the permanent expression of innocent query. But to others, they were windows to a vacant soul. The essence of his being had withdrawn so completely into itself that he no longer had access to it.

At first he was ravenous and was as much concerned with covering himself with his food as with eating it. They had to keep him away from water for he would drink copious amounts. It was thought he might have a diabetic condition, but this proved negative. In fact, apart from a sprained ankle, dehydration and near starvation, he was in tolerable physical shape. He was not violent but his behaviour tended towards certain predilections and his emotions seemed strictly controlled from outside himself.

He was kept in a darkened room for light hurt his eyes. The drapes were kept drawn but when the sun came around in the afternoon through a slit in the curtains, it threw a dazzle of sunlight in the middle of the floor. Mindlessly, he would move to lie in foetal fashion in the pool of light and like an old man in his dotage he groped for a familiar word. He would run his fingers around the random perimeter of the projected sunlight with an expression of searching. Searching for some fragment of connection to an understanding…to an understanding of an enigma which he had long forgotten.

For a week or two he was the talk of the town, but enquiries as to his identity led nowhere. Promising leads petered out; he remained a mystery.

In time, people forgot about him.

Other than his peculiar habits around food and water and his childish attraction to puddles of light, his behaviour, though strange, was benign and eventually an elderly priest took him in. He was looked after by the priest's housekeeper.

They gave him simple jobs around the church and of an evening, through several summers, he would sometimes be seen shuffling through the churchyard, for he walked with a slow scooter-like gait as a blind man might anticipate the edge of a precipice.

One afternoon, his body was found lying in the nave. He had fallen from a door in the bell tower carelessly left open. As the priest entered the church, it took him a moment or two to realize what he was seeing, for the crumpled body lay in a diffraction of brilliantly coloured light thrown by the sun from a round stained-glass chancel window. It was as though he were covered in psychedelic autumn leaves. The effect was quite beautiful.

Lifelike

After Fred Medicom's wife died, not having friends or relatives, he was lonely. He was too old, he thought, to change his habits. He couldn't tolerate having another person live with him and he doubted they would tolerate living with him. Browsing the internet, as he usually did for no particular reason, he stumbled upon "Love Dolls", the polite terminology for "Sex Dolls". These were life-sized dolls, made of all of the modern material to simulate a perfect woman, even down to the feel of flesh.

In particular he missed the feel of a warm body next to him when he would awaken in the night. This together with his loneliness was enough to overwhelm his common sense, to the absurdity of spending a mint of money to purchase Davinia.

Though she came in an unmarked box, he was embarrassed. "My son ordered it," he stammered when it was delivered by the Fed Ex man. "I've no idea what it is." The FedEx man smirked.

The box was heavy. He struggled to roll it up into the bedroom. He took her out of the box, laying her on his bed. She was all that she had been said to be. In fact, right then and there, her presence, dressed only in fundamental undies, began to affect him as if she were a real woman.

He had ordered the additional feature of heating so that when he awoke he would feel a warm body near him.

Davinia became much more than that to him. He made her his constant companion. He would sit her in the chair while he wrote. He would place her lounging on the chesterfield while he watched television. He would sit her in the car as though she were a passenger, sometimes leaving her for hours while he went about his business. He would stand her up so she could watch him at his work in his workshop, and in bed Davinia was helplessly at his pleasure. For a while, though she became his constant companion, he avoided taking her anywhere she might have been an embarrassment to him. The exception was when he met with his beer buddies, where, for a laugh, Davinia was their plaything.

A neighbour who regularly phoned him was the first to become suspicious. He hadn't answered the phone for some days. To see if he was alright, she went across to his house. The door was unlocked. "Mr. Medicom!" she shouted. Nobody answered. She went through to the kitchen. Seated at the kitchen table was a figure dressed in a bra and panties that she thought at first was a real woman. Then she screamed. Fred Medicom was lying face-down on the floor with several stab wounds in the middle of his back. A bloodied kitchen knife lay on the table next to Davinia.

The Green Eye of the Little Yellow God

"Man Killed by Tortoise", the *Star* headline read. Had it not caught my eye the name certainly would, for Jameison had once been my friend. It was a bizarre happening. We were fellow archaeologists. He was on a field trip in a part of the world where eagles frequently dropped turtles from a great height onto rocks to break their shells. A few inches to the left or right and it would have missed him.

I was not surprised at his death or the manner of his demise. Nor, in the light of recent happenings, will I be surprised at the manner of my own. You see, at this very moment, I am trapped in my wrecked station wagon hanging by a rear wheel from a high tension cable several hundred feet above Burlington Bay. It is dark but in the floodlights I can see the police and firemen, making preliminary efforts to land a man on the wagon, equipped with the Jaws of Life to cut me free. Why I am not electrocuted or at the bottom of Burlington Bay is a mystery which, in due course, I will try to explain. There is a strong smell of gasoline, but amazingly, I am quite cool and collected.

It is not easy to figure how all this came about but I suppose it started when Jameison and I were on our first postgraduate dig. It was in Iraq, not far from Mosul and in the vicinity of the Nineveh ruins. On the basis of our professor's research, there was the suspicion that a tomb might be found in an area that dated back to pre-biblical times. We were there all one summer and found very little; at least I thought we had found very little until one night when we were coming back on the boat, and Jameison pulled me into his cabin. He carefully unfolded the blanket and there it was. I was utterly stunned; it was absolutely magnificent.

Archaeologists are a serious lot and we were no exception. In keeping with the high principles of our scholarly backgrounds we were prepared for the simple artisanship of primitive peoples, even prepared to be amazed by their skills, but nothing in our extensive learning could have prepared us for what Jameison had just taken from the blanket. Sculpted from salmon-pink marble down to the last infinitesimal detail, it was simply incredible.

I didn't know whether to laugh or cry but then my reflexes decided it for me. Jameison and I rolled around that cabin until the tears ran down our cheeks, until out of exhaustion, we partially regained our sanity. Most primitive phallic symbols are no more than the vague idea of a linear rigidity that does little more than stimulate a vivid imagination, but not this one. The only decent way to describe it would be to say that it was the kind of protuberance that a mischievous Michelangelo might have sculpted for his embarrassed twelve-foot David if there had been a nude eleven-foot Daphne in the studio at the time.

"Where on earth did you get it?" I said.

"From the Nineveh dig. I found it on the last day at the ten-foot level," he replied.

"Why didn't you tell anybody?"

"What! And let those ruddy Iraqis have it? Not likely!"

We pondered the absurdity of how a relic that couldn't have been a day older than Late Renascence could have been found ten feet under the Iraqi desert. We might have saved our breath, for my guess is that even the best archaeological minds will not be able to throw light on its origins.

It was sometime after we got back to Toronto that bizarre happenings began to plague Jameison. Some were no more than silly or embarrassing, like those revealing Freudian slips that he kept making that alerted people to exactly what he didn't want them to think he was thinking at a precise moment when this would be enough to destroy a relationship. But many incidents were downright dangerous where Jameison seemed to be avoiding death by the skin of his teeth. For example, plate-glass windows had a habit of shattering when he was in the vicinity. Once he was precipitated out of a fourth floor window. Thank God, a canopy abutting the hotel entrance broke his fall. Things happened to other people too, when he was around. You very likely remember the incident of the meteorological balloon in the ladies' toilets at the CNE; it was in all the papers. Or that unfortunate business of the bishop's surplice and the swell-organ at that church in Don Mills.

Several weeks of this and Jameison was on the edge of a nervous breakdown. It began to dawn on him that his problems might result from the possession of the Nineveh phallus, so one night he went out and buried it in a farmer's field. If he thought he was accident-prone before, his life was sheer murder after. He became an absolute Jonah. Catastrophes happened by the hour, culminating at a public function when he shared the stage with the president of an early feminist movement and she spontaneously combusted. In desperation he went out and dug it up again, though it took him three days of sheer hell to find.

But he was an intelligent fellow and he figured if things turned for the worse when he got rid of it, they should improve if he stayed close to it, and this proved to be good logic. He began taking it around with him wherever he went. I was pleased to see that life went much smoother for him after that. Not that it was easy. It was pitiful to see the near panic in his eyes when he would find himself separated from it by a mere arm's length. The shape of the thing too, was so obvious. At first, he would wrap it in heavy brown paper. This worked fine, until with continuous handling, the paper would cling to its contours until its shape was as distinctive as if it were a trombone or a set of bagpipes. Everywhere he went people would stare at it with a kind bemused curiosity and the less mannerly would suffer the embarrassment of an uncontrollable fit of the giggles. Eventually, he was forced to have a wooden box made for it, which since it was sculpted out of solid marble with all the natural appendages, measured nineteen-and-a-half by seven by five inches and weighed thirty-two-and-a-half pounds. Of course, he dared not explain what was in the box and so he soon gained the reputation of an eccentric.

His life returned, more or less, to normal as long as every single place he went he lugged the box around with him, which invariably he did, even to the bathroom. Well, almost invariably. The one time when he was to forget, was crucial. Jameison had been courting Melissa Partington and they had been engaged for several months. It was on the occasion when he went to the Partingtons to discuss the wedding arrangements, and it is possible that it was the stress of the auspicious occasion that caused him to forget the box. It is not commonly known what the construction of the sentence was that he was using when a Freudian slip caused him to say knickers instead of vicars, but it was obvious that the unfortunate word gave a different and quite obscene meaning to what he had decently intended to say. A veritable avalanche of Freudian slips followed in his desperation to explain, but which simply compounded vulgarity upon vulgarity. Her parents were mortified and Melissa refused to speak to him ever again.

Several months later Melissa and I were married, and that was my mistake. Jameison felt I had taken advantage of him. Our relationship was never the same. We treated each other civilly but at a distance.

It was a month or two after the headline "Man Killed by Tortoise" appeared in *The Star* that I returned home from the University to find a letter from his executors. It told me I had been honoured by a small bequest. On the table was a box measuring nineteen-and-a-half by seven by five inches and weighing thirty-two-and-a-half pounds.

That was a couple of weeks ago. Life isn't easy but I manage. There was that embarrassing incident at my daughter's wedding that we managed to hush up. Melissa is threatening to leave me, and then of course there is tonight's fiasco. I was feeling around on the back seat of the wagon for that damned box when I remembered I had left it in Melissa's car. Then I felt the near-side wheel ride up onto the bridge abutment.

Ah! The first fireman has been lowered onto the station wagon. Oops! He has slipped, poor devil. I hope he's on a safety belt.

A Cock and Bull Story

Randy Mountford had badly underestimated Davenport. Thought him a nerd. Had bandied the intimacies of his affair with Davenport's wife Zenia around the office. He disliked the man with the contempt that jocks have for a puny physique. He wondered how Davenport had attracted Zenia in the first place. They had met when Davenport had been down in the Islands studying West Indian sorcery; Uredo, he called it. Can you imagine a real man wasting his time on that?

But she had been a good screw for a week or two until he tired of her and moved on. You can have her back, he had told Davenport in his office cubical on that afternoon. He liked to rub salt in the wound and was disappointed he couldn't get a rise out of him, for Davenport showed no reaction. He simply went on typing into his computer.

That night, Randy had settled in to watch the Monday night football game with a couple of cans of Moseley's Dark Ale when the pains started. It felt as though his feet were trying to burst out of his shoes. He barely got his shoes off before his feet swelled to several times their normal size. At the same time he seemed to be ballooning into his clothes. He ripped off his shirt, but before he could get out of his jeans the seams split. He was gaining bulk and weight rapidly. The couch collapsed beneath him. The side-table was knocked over. The beer went flying. He was indescribably hot. He blundered towards the door knocking over more furniture. His feet had now taken the form of hooves, and he was barely able to turn the doorknob before his hands took on a similar form. Coarse hair was growing all over his body and he was unaware he was sprouting horns.

His first reaction was that of acute embarrassment. He wanted to hide. It never occurred to him that he might have gone to the local hospital emergency department. He was now in the backyard on all fours with the remnants of his clothes falling off him. He clambered down the ravine that backed on to the house and clambering back up the other side, spent the night in total mental confusion standing in a field on the adjoining farm. It must be a nightmare, he agonized; any moment I shall wake up.

Tilly was first to notice, over breakfast. "Herb," she said, "there's a bull in the lower field." Herb Weirstein put on his coat and went out to look. Tilly was right. There was a bull in the lower field, and an angry bull at that. Herb couldn't figure out how he had gained a bull overnight. He checked with all the neighbouring farms. No cattle had gone missing. Finders is keepers, he thought. But this was a spirited bull. Nobody could get near it for the first few days.

It was frustrating for Randy. He wanted to say, "That effing bastard Davenport has changed me into an effing cow," but all he could utter was, "Mooooooo, mooooooo," and bellow and snort and paw the ground and charge at anybody who came near. For he thought of himself as a cow—a kind of reverse male chauvinism. Eventually they brought in the vet. When Randy came round, his nose was bloody and sore and he was tethered to a stake in the middle of the field with a rope through the ring in his nose.

The weeks passed. He was indescribably bored. Chewing cud was a poor substitute for the Saturday night booze-ups at McGillicuddies. He missed the darts, and at closing time, taking home Millicent... or Margaret... or Fiona... or Deirdre... or Daphne... or Jennifer... or he might get lucky and pick up a fresh bit of skirt. It didn't matter to Randy—another guy's wife, girlfriend, sister? There were Harrison Massey Ferguson seeders that hadn't sown as many wild oats. Even now, visions of his romps with Cassandra or Desiree or Albert Jones's wife Dinny or Bill Murphy's moll Esmerelda or that nurse that Jack Parsons knocked around with—what was her name? (she was quite a turn on, that one; what that girl couldn't do with her stethoscope)—filled his every waking hour and farmyard dream. He missed the smutty jokes, the hockey, the football, the nights out with the boys. He missed his frequent trips to Club Med. He missed strutting around swimming pools in a tan and his polka dot boxers. Above all, he missed the pursuit and conquest of women.

Now he was a constant round of eating, peeing and shitting. Even cows turned grass to milk. It seemed to him that he was useless to man and field.

He began to adjust to his new circumstances, though there were occasional setbacks. One day, Davenport and Zenia stopped by and stood looking over the fence at the far end of the field like the proverbial red rag. He forgot the ring, the rope and the stake, and charged. His nose was very sore for several days after that.

He could still see his house from the field. Sadly, one Thursday, he saw them loading his furniture into a van. He bellowed and snorted but nobody even glanced his way. He had noticed there had been considerable activity at the house for several days after he left. The police were puzzled. Obviously there had been an altercation—the smashed furniture, the torn fragments of his clothing. The best guess was that some cuckolded husband had taken revenge, but they couldn't find a body. Squads of volunteers beating the underbrush with sticks came within yards of him. "It's me, it's me!" he wanted to say. He was quite touched that they should be so concerned about him, and he couldn't help noticing there were some good-looking floozies amongst them. What wouldn't he give for a couple of hours with one, and he tried winking at one of the prettiest one. "There is something wrong with that cow's eye," he heard her say to her girlfriend. For although he had taken on the form of a bull, all his preferences remained those of a man. But the search parties came and went and nobody found a body and even Inspector Dobsby was totally flummoxed by the cow-pancake they had found on the back porch.

One morning, a month or two later, several farmers came into the field. Among them was Herb, and he recognized Jed Walcott from Chelmsley dairy farms. They prodded and poked him. "He looks sound enough, looks like a cross between a Guernsey and a Jersey—might fire up some good milkers," says Jed. "Tell you what, I've got a couple a cows up at my place need servicing. You wanna try him at that? We can keep him busy for life if he's any good."

"Suits me, Jed," says Herb. "I was going to have 'im put down... worth a few bucks at the knackers' yard... but if you think he might be useful? Why not—let's try 'im."

Randy understood that a new and important change had come over his life. He was going to have to dig down real deep. Randy realized that, from somewhere, he was going to have to find the same enthusiasm for cows that he'd had for women—he was going to have to put some of that good grass to use.

Duel in iPod Time
A short story in X fragments

I

Pericles is an unusual name, especially for someone who was not of Greek origin, but it served Robert well. It may have been why he had formed a close association with Robert Apaminondas who was not of Greek origin either. They came to be known as the two Roberts. They had other things in common. Both were unmarried. Both were loners. Neither had close family. Financially they had reached a time in life when, had they retired, they could have lived comfortably if not lavishly. Underlying their apparent contentment was a profound ennui not born of depression, but of the feeling that they had achieved most of what they considered important in life. Not friends but close acquaintances, they enjoyed a companionship comprised a routine of tennis on Wednesday mornings, and chess at each other's apartments on Saturday afternoons.

II

Once the issue had been decided, it became necessary to make elaborate preparations. For reasons that will be evident later, they did not wish the law to become involved. Both let it be known they would take a leave of absence for at least a year, perhaps two. Independently, they set up bank accounts so that, while they were away, their apartments might be maintained. At this time it was not certain that neither would be leaving or that both would be leaving or that one or the other would be leaving. It was only necessary that all of the eventualities be covered. Also, they pooled their remaining finances, opening an off-shore account under assumed names, an account that either one of them could access. In a roundabout way it was a wager.

III

The crux of the situation revolved around a unique coincidence. Neither was aware that the other was taking a holiday in France until they found themselves looking into the window of the same antique curiosity shop. After their initial surprise it became evident they were both interested in the same item: a magnificent set of 18th Century dueling pistols. Both had resolved to buy them, and so each paid half and they owned them mutually. Each would have possession of them for alternate weeks. Their chess meetings offered the opportunity for the pistols to change hands.

IV

Neither had ever fired a pistol before but possession of these antiques gave them the impetus to enquire further into the subject of dueling. The pistols were seductive and both found that merely handling them was almost erotic. They paced off in their rooms and struck the rituals, standing edgewise, shoulders back, one foot before the other in a stance that gave the slimmest of silhouettes to an opponent. When the decision was made, it was made without rancor and mostly out of desperation to relieve boredom.

V

They would observe the niceties. One difficulty was the need for seconds. Involving others would lead to unnecessary complication so they agreed to tape the countdown. 18th Century 'man about town' costumes were acquired from a local theatrical provider, each on his own credit card. Return of the costume(s) might prove to be unwise. The pistols were flintlock, still very functional, and came with six balls. Robert Two was a chemist, so black powder was no problem. One of them would take a spade and the other would take a rake.

VI

To arrive at dawn they traveled in one car to a clearing in a remote area of reforestation, changed into high-collared shirts, riding boots, fancy weskits, cravats and frock coats. Each took and cocked a pistol that was loaded beforehand. Robert One pressed play on the tape player at his feet. They stood back to back, pistols pointing to the sky, and waited, pacing only as the pre-recorded tape sounded: one, two, three, four, five, six, seven, eight, nine, ten. Turn, aim, FIRE! The reports were almost simultaneous. There would not have been time for either one to reconsider. Robert Two fell, by sheer luck, a ball straight to the heart at twenty paces, for both were novices. Fortuitous in a way for a non-fatal wounding requiring medical attention would have created a situation difficult to explain.

VII

Robert One dug down five feet and buried Robert Two, his clothes, the tape player, and the pistols, then spread the excess soil, and raked leaves over the newly turned earth. The place was seldom visited. Within a day or two no signs of disturbance would be visible.

VIII

Robert One let it be known he would not be taking a leave of absence. It was almost two years before cheques for Robert Two's utilities and apartment rental began to come back "insufficient funds". The landlord, to be on the safe side, did report to the authorities that his tenant Robert Apaminondas had not returned. What could the police do? The case, if it was a case, was almost two years old. This wasn't television, so there was no body, nor any concerns from relatives, nor any signs of foul play. The man could be whooping it up somewhere down in the islands. The report in the files comprised one sheet recording his disappearance.

IX

Robert One found a new tennis partner who also played chess and had a simple name: Robert Smith. Life was still boring. All that remained of the incident was a brief account in his diary that remained unread and was thrown out in the trash by a distant relative after his death 20 years later.

X

The end.

Virtual Virtuosity
(or Ingenious Genius?)

He found out quite by accident in a piano store. You know how you surreptitiously run your fingers over the keys, much as one might kick the tires on a used car. Anyway, to his absolute mind-boggling surprise, out came the first 15 bars of Chopin's *Revolutionary Étude*. Everybody in the store stopped to look and see who the brilliant pianist was. Even the manager came over and started to elaborate on the quality of that particular baby grand. Embarrassed, he quickly made some excuse to leave the store. He was badly shaken. You see, he had never studied music, never played a musical instrument, never touched a piano in his life.

At work on the following Monday he snuck into the school's music room where there was an upright. Careful to make sure nobody was about, he again ran his fingers over the keys. Out came Saint-Saëns' Piano Concerto No. 2 in G Minor from beginning to end, and to perfection.

Naturally, he bought a piano and had it delivered to his apartment. In the evenings he played to his heart's content... Debussy, Schubert, Schumann, Tchaikovsky, Satie, Liszt, Bach, and of course, Chopin—all the great composers for piano. But you can't keep something like this secret for long and, through a friend, he was heard by the music critic for *The New York Times*, who was staggered at his incredible ability to play all of the musical repertoire as expertly as any of the leading performers of the day.

In due course he got an agent who set up a series of concerts. His debut was slated for Carnegie Hall. There was one problem: when he would sit down at the piano, he had no idea what he was going to play. In fact, even when he was playing it, since he was not a classical music buff, he was often unaware of what he was playing. One expects a certain eccentricity where genius is concerned and so the PR people advertised the concert as a catch-as-catch-can, a potpourri. Whatever he played would be whatever he played.

The evening arrived. The novel approach worked well. The Hall was full. The lights dimmed, and to the applause of an expectant audience, he walked onto a stage where a thousand geniuses had walked before. Seating himself at the piano, he flicked his tails. Then bowing his head for effect he sat quietly for a moment or two. There was a hushed silence. He ran his fingers over the keys. He ran his fingers over the keys with greater vigour. He ran his fingers over the keys several times. Each time it sounded as if you or I had run our fingers over the keys. After a minute or so, he sensed the audience was becoming restless, an occasional cough, a community of clothing moving, the sounds sharpened by the acoustics.

He had one single thought of extraordinary clarity. It was that God must have a most mischievous sense of humour.

All That Glitters

We were barely into our teens, but beyond the stage when boys and girls are anathema to one another. Meg and I hit it off. Neither of us liked the city. Meg had a tiresome mother and my folks were seldom around, so whenever we could we would gather enough grub together for a few days and, literally, head for the hills. In addition to the Buick, my father had an old, old Ford that he never drove. I was under age, but what the hell!

    Some months before, we had stumbled on an idyllic spot, off the beaten track. It was a clearing that could be entered from only one direction on account of the terrain, and it was tucked in behind nearly impenetrable bush where nobody would ever find us. I recall one trip in particular. It was in the late afternoon. We were gathering flat stones to make a fire pit. Meg discovered a pile of them against the cliff face. As she removed them they started to reveal an aperture. We were intrigued, but it was almost dark so we decided to explore further in the morning.

    We were up early. Sure enough, as we removed more stones, an entrance was revealed, roughly the shape of a squashed semicircle, but by lying on our bellies we could wriggle through. Naturally it was dark inside, lighted only through the small access, but we could more than stand up, and to the extent that it amplified and echoed our voices we could tell we were in a large chamber.

It was to be our cave. We both determined not to reveal a word about it to anybody. On future trips we explored further, taking powerful flashlights. It turned out to be a huge cavern with entrances to other mysterious chambers that likely went on for miles under the hills. We were afraid to wander far from the entrance for fear of getting lost. Nobody would ever have found us. We were careful not to disturb anything, as there were bones about the floor and in an alcove were several human skulls.

On a wall were images of three silhouettes of the hands of two adults and a child. A most surprising find in an adjoining chamber was a small pile of gold nuggets—surprising, because there had never been evidence of gold in this area. When I look back, I marvel at how disciplined we must have been, for we both vowed never to touch the gold. We realized that if either of us was found with a gold nugget, it would set in motion an unstoppable chain of events that neither of us wanted. Whenever we left, we would carefully conceal the entrance with the stones.

All this happened many years ago. We grew up and we grew apart. Meg moved out west; I moved east. We lost touch. I doubt either of us has a yen to go back, for though there was a holiness about the place, there was also an eeriness. I recall we both commented that often we did not feel we were alone. Still, I keep a weather eye on the archeological press. So far, there has been no evidence of the cave's rediscovery. But I shall never forget the quiet stillness of this sanctum where it was always night.

Early Wheat

I knew I would eventually give in to a lifetime's temptation when, as a small boy, I innocently asked my grandfather, "Grandpa, what is *Hot Ice*?" He subtly changed the subject as a parent might when surprised by the question, "Mummy, Daddy, where did I come from?" But once privy to the lurid secrets of adolescence I soon learned what *Hot Ice* was, just as I learned about sex. Perhaps it was the euphoria it has in common with sex that fascinated me. Of course, euphoria is the culmination of sex, whereas, it is the beginning and the end of *Hot Ice*.

I sit at my rough bench looking at the flask of pink crystals I have created. In doing so, I have committed a criminal act punishable by summary execution in all of Earth's thirty-six segments.

Nobody remembers who coined the term *Hot Ice* but it is appropriate. How innocuous the crystals look, similar in appearance to crushed ice, but the colour of rose quartz. They do not melt like ice but evaporate slowly like naphthalene. The crystal surface has the appearance of giving off fluorescence, as though it were converting some proportion of ultraviolet to visual light. Instruments cannot measure this phenomenon. It is curious in that it also fluoresces without the presence of ultraviolet radiation. Any chemist with reasonable skills can make it from fairly common ingredients. It is assimilated through the skin so I am dressed in a composite suit, a mask, thick rubber gloves. As an extra safeguard, I breathe an outside air supply.

I took every precaution. Some years back, while out prospecting, I stumbled over a century-old mine. The shaft, driven horizontally through rock into a hillside, was dry and in good repair. Later, I remembered the place and purchased several thousand acres on which it stood. The entrance is well concealed, for nature has had a century or so to repair man's ravages. Logging and mining roads are long overgrown. It is miles from the nearest lake and not accessible by air. On foot is the only way in; it's a two-and-a-half-day hike through the bush. It took months of preparation to bring in supplies by backpack.

Hot Ice was formulated some forty years ago. At first it was difficult to figure how it had been made, since those who came into contact with it were in no condition to tell. Within minutes of touching a single crystal the victim became autistic and went into a euphoric stupor, totally incapacitated by waves of exquisite pleasure. In theory a piece of Hot Ice the size of a mothball could keep a group of people in this state for months or until it evaporated. In practice the victims died of dehydration within a few days, possessed by ecstasy of such intensity that they had no concern for eating, drinking or sleeping, yet would die blissfully, without the evident distress common to people who die of thirst. They would expire in a final rush of urgent orgasm, not survivable in its intensity. Gender and age were irrelevant to the outcome.

At first, doctors kept victims on intravenous, but they were so utterly pre-occupied they were of no more use to themselves or to others than if they had been in a coma. Some said you could twist a man's arm off when he was under the influence and he wouldn't flinch.

Withdrawal was unspeakable. Within hours the victims were in agony, which could not be relieved by the most powerful painkillers. After much soul-searching, the moral dilemma was partially solved by leaving them on the drug, to succumb to their absolute disregard for themselves.

There were attempts to commercialize the drug by the unscrupulous, to treat it as heroin or cocaine. The death toll was horrific. Figures were quoted at over thirty percent of all under-eighteens. Populations were decimated, until rigid measures, the "Rapture Squads", and inflexible laws administered with immediacy reduced the problem to an occasional and well-publicized outbreak.

I have no plans to do anything with the crystals. I am simply curious to see what they look like and to experience the thrill of the precarious position I find myself in. Taking the flask, I carefully pour the crystals into a much smaller vial, which is corked and sealed; then I place it in a padded ammunition box salvaged from several wars ago. Padlocking the box, I pick up the miner's lamp and make my way into the intestines of the mine where I bury the box under a pile of tailings. Then taking all evidence of the crystal manufacture, I bury it several hundred yards from the mine entrance.

Tomorrow I shall make my way back south to the city.

II

This evening I watch from the third floor, corner window, of the best of the rooms in Mrs. MacDonald's boarding house, having risen from the dingy basement through a disorderly ascent of lesser rooms, which in one way or another, were vacated by her tenants. The terrifying uncertainty of survival keeps depression at bay during the day, but as the evening descends, waves of sad anxiety sweep over me until I am a procession of half-formed thoughts beachcombing a desolate shore awaiting the tide of merciful sleep. It is difficult to sleep for the noise, as building after building crumbles.

Before me stretches a city thoroughfare subjected to the accelerated ravages of time, as though history came too quickly for it. The wreckage of rusting cars lies casually about the cityscape. The buildings, like carious teeth, barely stand, in a scene crocheted together by the vigorous infiltration of grey powdered silica, finer than sand. There are no grasses, no plants, not even weeds. The vista is swathed in bland neutrality of non-colour more arid than ash. The essence of life has evaporated from every particle. Coke from coal, gradual relentless disintegration; the molecular structure settling as in an accelerated hourglass. It is frightening to look upon the world as others might see it a hundred thousand years from now.

Down one side of the street two men approach each another. They move with a shuffling gait. Each pushes one foot ahead, making sure it is on firm ground before taking his weight off the other foot. They inch along keeping a determined grip on the remains of the buildings' facade. The occasional structure is still standing and now and then one of the men will disappear, reappearing after a minute or two carrying, if his scavenge has been successful, a morsel of food.

The men meet each other. Both keep finger holds on the frontage of a partly demolished building. They do not speak but, as if meeting on a cliff face—ludicrously, for they appear to be on solid ground—one tentatively gropes around the other for a handhold on the far side. Neither will let go with both hands. They execute this peculiar manoeuvre until they are safely past each other.

The man walking away is swallowed by the approaching dusk. The other, walking towards me, I watch surreptitiously through a chink in the drapes. I listen to see if he will enter my building, but he is on the far side of the street. To cross without a structure to hang on to would be risky. Nevertheless, I eye the shotgun standing in the corner.

It is of no consequence that I should spend yet another evening alone.

The first evidence of dissolution was some twenty years ago, sometime after the discovery and the scourge of *Hot Ice*. Changes must have been happening long before we ever realized. Events which cannot be explained by nature have often been considered magic. Much of the entertainment industry back in those days owed its success to the staged miraculous. So it was not surprising when a gradually increasing number of people claimed experience of the supernatural. At first, they were not taken seriously. It was the very gradualness of it that made the change so difficult to detect. Statistics, like averages, owe a debt to the future and a certain amount of faith in them over time is necessary if they are to be believed. But eventually the alarming frequency of these unexplainable events was impossible to ignore. A virus was suspected a virus that affected the brain. Government money was diverted and many promotions were mounted to raise money in an effort to track down the mysterious cause, but without success.

Even when groups of people could corroborate each other's accounts of strange happenings, many put this down to mass hysteria. Some suggested ergot was responsible—the grain fungus that drove peasants mad in the Middle Ages. Never before had the press given such a confusion of opinions. Governments, as usual, steadfastly denied the obvious. On the other hand, experts from all fields—astronomers, astrologers, clairvoyants, and various scholars of the paranormal and even a few physicists—came up with theories, none of which could be proved.

My first untoward experience was more bizarre than frightening. I remember it as though it were yesterday though it was seventeen years ago. One evening I was reading in bed, when in an instant, a woman appeared beside me. There was no commotion, no bouncing of springs, suddenly she was just there; we were both flabbergasted, but then she gathered herself and screamed. It is curious the idiotic thoughts you have at such times. My concern was how I might explain her to my landlady. But the problem resolved itself when the woman leapt out of bed, took several steps across the room, and disappeared.

I sat for a minute or two on tenterhooks. Had Mrs. MacDonald heard her scream? But the threshold of ambient sound—the passing traffic—must have muted the sound or perhaps everyone upstairs was already asleep.

The humdrum of my daily routine had been shattered. My mind was now filled with fragments of possibility, which by rational process I could not piece together. It was almost dawn before I fell asleep.

The experience made me sympathetic to events, which by now were reported frequently on television and in the press. At that time, many of us had experiences beyond explanation. Most of us kept quiet for fear we should be considered, at the very least, neurotic.

The disappearances, too, must have been happening all along. Before the turn of the century, people disappeared in politically unstable countries and even in democracies. Such disappearances were usually the result of criminal activity, particularly sexual crimes leading to murder. It was the gradual increase in these disappearances, which in the beginning made it difficult for us to realize that these happenings were for a quite different reason.

Then there were the cases of amnesia. A rash of people would find themselves in other places, sometimes halfway round the world, without the least idea of how they got there. Children, unaware of where they came from, could not be returned to their families. Whole television channels communicated details and photographs of lost ones. Families sat in relays peering at the screen hour after hour. Children began to wear identity tags. The fabric of society began to fray.

My first inexplicable experience was benign. To have found myself in bed with a woman might be thought the answer to a bachelor's prayer. My second was terrifying.

The agency had landed a big account. The gathering was festive. The meal at Casey's was sumptuous and the wine overflowed. It was after midnight when I left the subway to walk, a little unsteadily, to Mrs. MacDonald's boarding house. I let myself in quietly by the side door and tiptoed down the basement stairs. As I reached the bottom stair, it gave way under my foot. I knew I could not have fallen far; I was only nine inches above the cellar floor, I thought. In an instant, the lower half of my body plunged into the void. I was hanging precariously from the bannister. A vicious, icy wind lashed my legs. Looking down I could see a murderous landscape—a mountaintop swathed in swirling snow. I felt the wind whipping my trouser legs and driving the sleet into my flesh, yet I could hear nothing. The stairwell remained in quiet darkness, nor did the brilliance of the blue mountain-light spill into it from the awful vista below. I was split between two worlds. I prayed the bannister would hold and desperately pulled myself up the stairwell. The void closed as soon as my legs were clear of it.

At first, I could not bring myself to let go of the bannister. My legs were freezing and my trousers wet. As the snow melted in the heat of the stairwell, I touched the stairs tentatively with my foot. They were again quite solid. Still I could not bring myself to let go of the bannister. I was some time pulling myself together. Afterwards, when I had to negotiate those stairs, it was with difficulty. I had lost my nerve. The next morning the events of the previous evening were the first thing that entered my mind. I put off looking out into the hall until after I had showered, shaved and dressed. I opened my door, and leaned across to establish a good grip on the bannister, then manoeuvred my way on to the stairs. The carpet was still wet.

It was about this time that I began to appreciate the malignancy of the problem. I remembered a vision from the night before; huddled together on the summit of that mountain was a wretched group of people dressed in summer clothes.

After that I asked Mrs. MacDonald for another room. She gave me Swenson's, who had not returned after a business trip. So I graduated to the second floor at the back.

I was beginning to understand why people were disappearing. If they slipped through a crack in space to some other part of the globe and landed amongst human habitation, they might not know where they were and might think they were suffering from amnesia, but at least the adults could get back unless they landed in wilderness, where they would drown, freeze, starve, or die of thirst.

It was a year or two after the turn of the century when structures started to collapse. In the beginning, it was thought these disasters were the result of terrorism. But failing structures gradually increased and when some years later, shortly after lunch on a Wednesday, the Empire State Building collapsed with massive loss of life, it began to dawn on us we were at the mercy of an unexplainable force.

Shortly after, the Channel Tunnel collapsed, followed by the Sydney Harbour Bridge, and soon almost every city, town, or village was saddened by similar calamities.

World economies were crumbling. Many insurance companies and banks had gone bankrupt. Production was beginning to suffer everywhere. The work force and the means of production were becoming more chaotic as hundreds of thousands disappeared and almost as many more were displaced. Factories and offices continued to collapse. Food production was down. Only through our diminishing numbers did we avoid worldwide famine.

Nobody understood what was happening. For the first time in history the world was struck by an impartial series of catastrophes; the strong were as vulnerable as the weak, the rich as impotent as the poor.

The people of the world who were left were polarized. The idealists, who thought the world made by God for mankind, naturally considered our misfortunes chastisement for sins. A great resurgence of fundamentalism gave the devil a profile he had not known since the Middle Ages. The materialists, who thought they were but another species, albeit superior, and who happened by accident of nature, to have inhabited the planet, still believed there was a logical explanation. In terms of the world we knew, both would be proved wrong.

I met Sven Sundin one morning on Prospect Street. He was expensively dressed, though his suit was filthy and he wore no shoes. In fact, he looked as if he had been dragged through a swamp. I wondered why he was wearing a ridiculous leather briefcase on his head. He was clearly on the verge of collapse. The boarding house was a short walk. I took the poor fellow with me.

By now I had graduated to the third floor front, Thurman's old room.

Since Mrs. MacDonald's disappearance I had bought a hotplate. Even the odour of lightly-browned toast would have brought her knock of disapproval on my door. But now I could do as I liked. Sundin was starving. I heated cans of stew. He ate ravenously, finishing off the stew and another can of beans and several cups of freshly brewed tea. The grub and the tea revived him. Soon he was telling me his story which, were it not for my own experiences, I would not have believed.

He was a civil engineer in Stockholm. About a week ago he had left his apartment at the usual time to go to work. He was on his way to the underground parking lot to pick up his car when, inexplicably, he found himself floundering in the sea. He could swim, so instinctively he began to tread water. He still had his briefcase with him, which contained important papers for a meeting later that morning; this he balanced on his head hoping he could keep the contents dry. Looking around he could see in the distance a beach with stringy palm trees. After swimming for some twenty minutes he felt the coarse sand of the beach under his feet.

He was on a hot sandy spit of land under a clear blue sky. He assumed he was in the tropics but had no idea of how he came to be there. The last he remembered was walking down to the underground garage. He was still wearing the business suit and carrying his briefcase. The time by his watch was eight-thirty, the date December 8th. This was about the time, and precisely the date, he had set out to pick up his car. He was relieved to learn that whatever had happened to him was not a memory problem. But his relief was short. He realized he was poorly equipped to survive in the wilderness, beautiful as it was. He was doomed unless he could reach habitation.

Tangled jungle came down to the water's edge. After a kilometre or two he came to a waterfall emptying into a cool, clear pool. He had refreshed himself, torn off his jacket and tie, and floated in the cool water. It was an idyllic spot. He could have languished there for hours were it not for a weight of anxiety, for he knew he had to move on. He had thrown away the papers and made a crude sun hat out of the soft leather briefcase. The jungle was impenetrable. He had walked along a shore that seemed endless. He walked for several days without food, though fresh water was plentiful. One night he was trapped part way up a cliff by the tide. He told me of many horrors, of reptiles, scorpions and of scrabbling land crabs that kept him from sleeping. He saw no sign of civilization until the fifth day, when on the far side of a crescent-shaped bay a kilometre or so distant, he saw two figures and a fishing boat pulled up on the beach. Shouting and waving his arms, with the last of his strength he broke into a shambling run, fearful the boat would put to sea. Near exhaustion, he had approached the fishermen, who by now had seen him, then he stumbled and fell, not on to the soft warm sand he had expected, but onto hard pavement.

From his description I gathered he must have landed in the alley behind the Sheraton Hotel. He had then wandered on to Prospect Street where I had found him dazed and confused.

The food and drink revived Sundin. His first concern was how he might return to his wife and family. Flying was hazardous. The disintegration of matter was not limited to bridges and buildings; cars were falling apart, and judging from the numbers of flights not reaching their destinations, so were aircraft. The very molecular adhesion was failing.

I loaned him money, and arranged to take him to the airport first thing the following day. But Sundin disappeared again as suddenly as the woman had.

The aberrations increased exponentially. The disintegrations random as fireflies flashing in the dark. The world was a black chaos of events, each catastrophe, in miniature, magnified in the particular by its effect on the individual, the family, and the community. Loneliness piled upon loneliness; grief compounded with interest. On the ragged minds of those who were left were only questions. But God did not choose to give a reason and man could not. Faith, science and myth all failed, but still the frantic search for answers continued. Some culled fragments of purpose from unsubstantiated theories. Others vacated the discomfort of their minds.

The relentless disintegration of structures, the terrifying experiences, the displacements of those who disappeared, and the terror of those who for the moment were left, gradually increased.

Benjamin Pascalia was the first to claim pi was no longer even approximately 3.14159. At first he was not believed. Science was in confusion. Faced with concrete evidence of the impossible, it fared worse than faith, for thrown back into the fictions of its own impossibilities, it was indistinguishable from faith. Eventually, Pascalia was vindicated. Pi was found to vary by more than one decimal place, depending upon where the calculation was carried out. Mathematicians soon discovered that other formulae pertaining to space were similarly changed and no longer reliable. Hypotheses on how the universe came about theorize that, at the time of the Big Bang, there were at least ten dimensions. Why the universe is set in three dimensions is a puzzle. But it is certain that our mathematics are good only for a three-dimensional world. We began to understand the calamity we faced. Earth was shifting dimension.

I owe my own survival to an observation I made some months ago. I noticed a brick was less stable than a sponge. Hard substances were more unstable than soft. People wearing hard leather soles were more vulnerable than those wearing running shoes. I devised a means of travel using two lengths of carpet which, in turn, I roll out in front of me and roll up behind. The others think I am mad.

Night is falling. The ground is shaking from the supernatural demolition of buildings. In the distance I can see the flashes of lightning storms. I shall finish off my last bottle of Scotch and read a chapter or two of Jerome K. Jerome's *Three Men in a Boat* before turning in. Tomorrow, I shall make my way back north to the mine, travel, with my carpets, a three-hundred-kilometre battlefield of imminent destruction. It has been over twenty years since I made up the batch of *Hot Ice,* and every day I have had to face the most insidious and powerful temptation I have ever known. If the mine is still there and if by a miracle I reach it, I shall at last tip the contents of the vial into the palm of my hand and deliver myself into the oblivion of pure ecstasy.

III

"Does it bother you, playing God, Xanicus?" said Commander Ebic pouring them both a glass of a particularly fine Earth-wine vintage.

"I'm used to it. I must have done several hundred planet dimensional de-constructions or Di-De-Cons as we call them."

"This is only my fifth," continued Ebic, "I can never get used to the savagery of it. You have got to admit, it is cruel."

"Is that our fault?" Commander Xanicus replied. "We did give them the drug. What could be more humane than pleasure so exquisite they wouldn't even know they were on the way out?"

"You mean *Hot Ice*, of course. But they wouldn't take it would they?"

"No, they wouldn't take it—at least most of them wouldn't. Was the triumvirate mad about that? I'd say! The expense was all they could think of—all that energy and time to Di-De-Con them. But they should not have been surprised. It is the weakness of this particular strain. Give them an immediate threat to their existence and they will fight like demons. Yet they are insensitive to the indulgence in an immediate gratification that will render the planet uninhabitable for their grandchildren. Curiously, this species has free will only as individuals; they do not have it as a group.

"They tell me we have tinkered with the genes of the new strains in a way that should resolve the problem. That is to say, make them more responsive to the long-term damage of their short-term actions. Perhaps shave a touch off their inflated sense of their own infallibility; genetically speaking, take a little of the God out of them.

"But once a planet reaches the point of no return and it is obvious that eventually it will no longer sustain primates of higher intelligence and can no longer meet the prime directive, it makes good sense to plow in the old crop and re-seed.

"If you are taking your ship back directly, will you take them my report? It merely outlines the near completion of the project. Within an Earth year or two we shall be down to the sub-particle base. I have told them they can send Vanicular out to start re-dimensioning very shortly. Then we just re-seed with the improved strain. I shall continue to orbit this planet—what do they call it... ?"

"*Uranus,*" Ebic offered.

"Yes, Uranus! I shall continue to orbit Uranus, beyond Earth's sensors of course, keeping an eye on the de-dimensional irradiators until Vanicular arrives."

"I suppose you are right, Xanicus, I mean about re-seeding, and I will report on your progress. But Xanicus, do you remember those plantings with the earlier strain—the one where the offspring lay around smelling flowers? They could hardly stir themselves to procreate, let alone meet the prime directive. Even those aphrodisiacs we engineered into the apples scarcely solved the problem."

"Of course I remember, Ebic. Earth was seeded with them. Fortunately, they were not too much of a problem; when we realized they were inferior, we re-seeded over them with the current crop in which we had upped the ambition and indulgence. It quickly crowded out the earlier strain. Why do you ask?"

"Well, when I was down on Earth at the pre-planning stage, I found that they held that first seeding in great esteem. *Adam and Eve in the Garden of Eden* they called it. In fact, they considered the grace of that state as being superior to their own. Were you aware of that Xanicus?"

"No, but it really does not surprise me when I think of the mess they have worked themselves into. Look, Ebic, don't get down on yourself. In a few millennia you will come back this way and look down on a Stone Age, a Bronze Age or an Iron Age and you will think to yourself what a great job we have done here today. Mark my words: this improved strain will meet the requirement perfectly."

"I hope you are right, Xanicus. Pity we can't see the downside of fiddling with the gene pool until it is too late."

"Of course I'm right, Ebic. Here's to your trip home. Cheers!"

"Ciao, Xanicus!"

Father's 2x4 by 8 Foot Cedar Stud

In his gut, he felt his breakfast digesting. The screwdriver in his hand was for slotted heads, while the screw, barely started, in the center of the eight-foot, two-by-four cedar plank, had a Robertson head. He turned on the ball of his foot as he had seen Michael Jackson do on many occasions and paced off the three and one half steps to his tool cabinet. It was blue, not dissimilar in color to the vase on the bedside table in Van Gogh's famous painting of his room. As his fingers curled about the drawer-pull, he felt his palmaris longus and flexor carpi stiffen as the drawer opened to its stop. On the right was an assortment of pliers. On the left was a selection of screwdrivers. He replaced the slotted driver in its allotted space and picked up a green-handled Robertson. Then, in a movement precisely the reverse of the drawer-opening, he closed the drawer, and turning on his heel as he had seen Peter O'Toole turn in *Lawrence of Arabia*, he repaced his steps.

His father had liked the smell of cedar. And in the early days, when they were mired in the lethargy of happiness, he would take the children out to the workshop. He could still remember his father's words as he and his brothers clustered about the cedar two-by-four. "That's none of your peelie-wallie white eastern cedar," he would say. "That's full-blooded western red." And lovingly he would run his hand the length of the flower-pot red stud, marveling at the scarcely visible grain with not a single knot from end to end. "Smell that," he would say, shoving his kids' heads towards the plank, and in turn, they would take deep long thoughtful sniffs until their mucus membranes felt as if lined by rough sandpaper. As he approached manhood he realized that he owed his love of cedar entirely to his father.

But his mother and father were having problems and there were constant arguments. He agreed implicitly with both of them and so could never figure out what they were arguing about. However, one morning his father left for work and did not return.

Those were difficult days—his mother trying to raise four young children. At times, in the jitters of tribulation when he felt particularly low, he would slip away to the workshop and run his hand up the cedar plank (as far as he could reach) just as his father had done. Lowering his voice by two octaves he would say to himself, "This is none of your peelie-wallie white eastern cedar; this is your full-blooded western red." Then he would sniff, taking in the dusky red fragrance, until his head was filled with sawdust.

Now, he was about to desecrate the stud. In fact, he had already measured four feet from one end and two inches from one edge and drilled a pilot-hole, which he had further countersunk for the head of the screw. The screw stood half a turn into the hole.

Though he loved his mother, he had realized lately that she was a jealous woman and would have regarded his father's whim for the cedar plank as other women might have reacted to their husbands had they taken a mistress. With maturity, his opinion of his father had changed too. For he now understood that it must have been heartbreaking for him to leave without taking the plank with him. Now, he saw his father's sacrifice as an expression of love. As with his father, lumber had been his life. He had not the slightest interest in girls, but notwithstanding cedar, the feel of a well-planed piece of pine or spruce with perfectly countersunk screws, was something else.

Standing before the bench he balanced his weight evenly over each foot. He could feel his gastrocnemius flexing behind his right knee in the give and take with his vastus lateralis. Leaning forward he placed the miniature square on the end of the screwdriver into the socket of the screw. Then he stood quite still, in complete silence, pondering. To a casual observer it might have appeared he had changed his mind, but that was not so. Laying the screwdriver on the bench, he pivoted on the fourth toe of his right foot. Walking past the tool cabinet, he stopped at five and one half paces, in front of a single sheet of paper held to the wall by push-pins in colours identical to those of Michelangelo's Sistine Chapel ceiling.

Taking his left index finger, he ran it down the left-hand column of the sheet of paper, stopping at the word *"Screw"*. Then, taking his right index finger, he ran it across the headings until it came to the word *"In"*. Moving his left index finger to the right and his right index finger down the page, his fingers converged on the word *"Clockwise"*. Never commit to memory anything you can look up, his father and Albert Einstein had drummed into him.

He turned about smartly just as he had seen Jeanette MacDonald turn after she had slapped Nelson Eddy, and resolutely made his way back to the bench. This time, without hesitation, he again inserted the small square on the end of the screwdriver. Slowly, deliberately and clockwise, he began to turn the screw.

A Visit with My Grandfather

They would have named it Devil's Island were the name not already taken. No place on Earth came closer to the myth of the netherworld than that forsaken place. But he was there, and that made it, for me, a fragment of heaven.

Imagine a void in the mind which the tapestry of ancestry and the community of family should have filled—a void where the history of a country should have served as a child's familiar. Imagine a mind where the word *belonging* had no meaning. Those were the things lacking in me. Perhaps it was why I yearned to walk in the footsteps of my grandfather.

My mother died when I was born. I never knew my father. I doubted my mother knew him very well. They shipped me from town to town, country to country, continent to continent, and eventually, hemisphere to hemisphere, until Dr. Bernardo's Homes lodged me, for the better part of my youth, with several farmers. And even then, I was moved from farm to farm. Enslaved might have been a better word, but I held no grudge.

I learned of my grandfather by the slimmest of chances, a chance so slim as to be suspect of being supernatural. While looking for unrelated information, a microfiche of the front page of a 1912 newspaper came out of nowhere. It remarked on the village, half a world away, in which I was born. A photograph caught my eye depicting the unloading of corpses onto a rickety pier. "Bodies Returned to the Mainland" the caption read. In the column listing the dead was a man with my mother's maiden name. Further enquiry confirmed I had found my grandfather.

I booked passage south on an ore carrier out of Halifax. The sea was no stranger. When people failed me, the sea was my comfort.

There were more difficulties than I had anticipated. Landing on the island was forbidden by the New Zealand Department of Internal Affairs. On the chart was the admonishment: *Shipping Stay Clear. Lethal Emissions.* A dotted line indicated the limits of the approach. I tried to arrange for fishermen to take me. Too risky, they said. But it was more than the danger. Nobody would talk about the island. There was a superstition about it.

A more seaworthy boat would have been available from one of the larger harbours, but I avoided making my intentions obvious, telling them I merely wanted to do a spot of offshore fishing. The boat was of surprising displacement to have been found in a Maori village. Not that it was much of a boat—a double-ender, clinker-built, gaff-rigged with a small jib and a motor that might have been handed down from the *African Queen*. Red sails had patches on patches. The shrouds were suspect. The running rigging was aging sisal. How it would perform in any kind of heavy weather, subjected to my limited sailing skills, did not bear thinking about. The owner probably shared my view. He had taken my last cent as deposit.

An hour before dawn I was a mile offshore, provisioned for four days. My minimal navigational skills that dictated I set course by dead reckoning—by my compass carefully corrected to the appropriate magnetic deviation. My scant knowledge of tides and currents I had picked up from local fishermen. I had a sixty-mile run before the wind with an estimated arrival of late afternoon based on an average of five knots. If I missed the island, my next landfall would be several weeks away, if at all. Precise navigation was not critical. The island rose some two thousand feet above the sea. The plume of gases and gray ash spewing from its summit would be easily visible at thirty miles. The forecast was promising. I would be fine as long as the weather held.

Several days before, I had flown over the island in a Fox Moth. This was long before tourists and the comfort of Cesnas. I knew a little of what to expect—a dot in the ocean that as I flew closer became a cauldron of molten lava.

Around noon and dead ahead, I saw the expected confusion of cloud close on the horizon. I was on course. The breeze was still blowing from astern. It must continue to do so, for I could only approach from windward. My destination was the southern edge of the island. Barely perceptibly throughout the afternoon, the island gradually replaced the ocean until the boat was in the lee of its shadow. A threshold of sound from the interior increased as I approached. The distant roar overwhelmed the sound of waves lapping at the cliffs. I sought the small break in the otherwise sheer lava which, on and off for centuries, had flowed into the sea. The anchorage was a shallow basin. I pulled the boat up onto coarse volcanic sand.

With the roar in my ears, I made my way along a half-mile of rough track leading up and over a crater wall. I stood transfixed at the panorama. I was looking down into the antithesis of life. Before me was a caldera in lifeless tones of ochre-gray. The life force was no match for this arid desolation. Nowhere did a touch of green, a single blade of grass, challenge the tyranny of this exuberant grave. Sulpataras exhaled sulphurous fumes, each orifice salted with deposits of chlorides:

ferric, ammonium, aluminium, sulphates: gypsum, alumite and alum. The heat through the soles of my boots from magma scant feet beneath the rock warmed my feet. The air was a yellow fume burning in my throat. Everywhere, the pale lemon of native sulphur tinged the solitude. Was this the crucible from which the ancients had contrived their vision of hell? Off to the left, fifteen hundred feet above, the mother-vent sounded the persistent moans of souls in torment. In the middle distance were the miners' quarters I had come half the world to see.

I crabbed my way down the crater wall, carefully avoiding conglomerations, slip-sliding my way through the loose lapilli until I reached the ruins. Ghostly and petrified cast concrete walls stood... but little else. Everything looked to have been dipped in yellow-gray mud and allowed to harden. I looked for the familiar and found a tap, a length of pipe, a kitchen pot, and outside on the rough road, a hitching post. Thick encrustation gave everything the look of children's stuffed toys.

On a flat slab of lava, I smoothed the drawings given to me by the Department of Mines. I was poring over them looking for the location of the workings when I felt his presence at my shoulder. I was neither frightened nor startled. The visions and the voices had come to me many times, but this was different. Usually they were strangers. I knew this man. This man knew me.

As though he guessed I was looking for the workings, he beckoned me to follow. Surefooted, he set off in the direction of a lower segment of the crater rim while I stumbled along behind.

He could have given me a half-dozen years. His hands were calloused and rough, his arms muscular. He resembled an Edwardian night watchman. He wore hobnailed boots, trousers of rough serge, shapeless and tied below the knee. He wore a union shirt, without a collar, and over it, a weskit. A watch fob hung from his weskit pocket. Round his neck was a neckerchief, and on his head, a well-worn bowler.

Only a heavy moustache, tobacco stained, separated him from my time.

With an effort he raised his voice over the threshold of sound. His eyes were slits, as though the noise bothered him. His accent was softly English, giving his e an eee sound. His *yes* came out as *yis*. *Every* became *Eevery*.

"It all happened here," he said, pointing to the mound of debris where the crater wall had collapsed. "We were taking out forty tons a week in the best of times. Forty tons of high quality rock-sulphur." He picked up a brownish-coloured encrustation the size of a kaiser roll. Heat had affected the outer skin. He broke it open and handed it to me. Inside was a pale yellow powder that stuck to my fingers like pollen. "We knew the cliff was unstable. We were planning to move to new diggings. We thought we could safely mine a few more tons. There were fourteen men and a boy under there." He pointed to the fall of tephra. "Some of us are still there."

It was difficult to speak over the roar. I said little. He was telling me all I wanted to know—showing me all I wanted to see.

He walked me back to the ruin of the miners' quarters. The drone of sound from the cone had changed ominously. We looked up from the shuddering ridge to see the immense plume of gases swirling about the rim of the sprue. "The wind is shifting. You had best be leaving," he said, looking at his watch. "By nightfall the wind will have come around," and turning to me, he handed me the watch. "You have it. I want you to have it."

"I can't take this. No! No! I can't take this," I stammered. "You will need it." I tried to hand it back to him but he had turned away and was already walking towards the buildings. Without looking back, he signified with a wave of his hand that the discussion was at an end. "I'll come back!" I shouted.

I barely heard his voice over the mounting roar, "No, don't come back! My work is done!"

I dared not linger. The crater was taking on a deadly haze. Fifteen hundred feet above, whimsies of electric-blue gases were pirouetting down the steep sides of the lava dome. I slipped the smooth cool silver of the watch into the inner pocket of my anorak, and turning, scrambled up the crater rim, then hurried down to the shore.

Within minutes, the boat was underway on a heading south. There was no need of a precise bearing. Close to due south would strike the north shore. Several times I looked back and saw him watching from the crater rim—a solitary figure in a bowler hat standing quite still. Then the need to trim the jib distracted me and when I turned to look again, he was gone.

I watched the island dwindle in the distance until it was swallowed by the sea. I watched the sky's reflection dying in the ocean's lie until it was swallowed by the night—the darkest night and the brightest stars I had ever seen. On a broad-reach the boat leaned into the footsteps of a steady breeze. Blocks squeaked and rattled as the sheets ran. Rigging groaned like an old man. Water slapped and dabbled as the bow sliced the placid sea, and the boat's wake had culled opalescent colours from rainbows.

I lay back and stared into the coal-black bowl—the pinpoint-porous backdrop of the sky filtering the sunshine days of a billion stars. Rigil Kentaurus and Beta Centauri pointed the Southern Cross. The star cloud constellations of my boyhood enforced an order on the randomness. Yet, I was lonely for north, for the Little Bear and the Sailor's Star. I sat huddled in the stern, with barely a finger on the tiller; I thought of the prospect of children and of grandchildren. I thought of how they might look back—of how I might now look back upon the lineage of Man stretching into de la Mare's *Dim Eden*. In the velvet darkness of the summer's night, I became part of the glorious immortal pageant, and God cradled me in his hands.

At first light I waited for landfall to force its wedge between the sea and sky. Presently I saw the singular hill marking the entrance to my anchorage. Downwind, I pushed hard on the tiller and close-reached to make the leeward mark at the river's mouth. Then reaching the dock, I luffed and lowered sail.

I felt in my pocket for my grandfather's timepiece, to see what time I had made. In my palm was a crushed and encrusted blob of metal, charred and tarnished beyond semblance; time had betrayed time.

Returning the treasured remnants to my pocket, I stepped ashore. I was ready to inherit the Earth.

What Heaven is Like

You know how it feels when you are coming out from under an anesthetic? It was like that. A voice from nowhere saying, "Mr. Whoeveryouare, it's all over. Wake up, wake up. Are you alright?"

"I think so, though it was a lot hotter than I thought it would be and I don't remember anything after I'd cooled down and they were raking out my ashes. I'm not sure, if I had it to do it over again, that I would go for cremation."

"Don't knock it," the voice said. "Try lying around in a cold, damp coffin for a couple of days. That's not fun either. But, either way, it's never worse than a root canal job."

By now I was beginning to gather my wits. "But where am I?" I said, beginning to get a handle on the image of the fellow I was talking to. He was about my age, though for the life of me, at that moment, I couldn't figure out how old I was. A pleasant enough fellow dressed in jeans and a tee shirt.

"You are in Heaven."

I'm in Heaven, I mused and the tune came immediately to mind. I wasn't entirely surprised; though not God's gift—heaven knows I left an absolute plethora of sins of omission—on the other hand, I wasn't an axe murderer or anything like that and I figured that if I didn't make the cut, that other place was going to be mighty crowded.

"But it looks exactly the same as Earth," I said.

"It might look like it but it isn't. The Old Man didn't make the same mistake twice. It's all think now... it's all about think."

"The Old Man?"

"God," he said. "We call him the Old Man. He doesn't mind. Realized he'd made a heck of a mistake with creating Earth. Part of it was the time restraints. You couldn't do a job of that size in six days. He realized within weeks what was the matter, and it was the matter."

"It was the matter?" I queried.

"Yes you know, matter... things, items, stuff, dirt, custard, slime, lettuce, diapers, rocks, jungles, even water, smoke and kapok and especially flesh. He noticed they couldn't leave matter alone, hoarding it, stealing it, coveting it (especially flesh), and even breaking it down to its tiniest parts and making big bangs out of it. So he made Heaven without matter. It's all ethereal. It's all think. Here in Heaven, you just think it, and it is."

I began to appreciate the incredible potential and harked back to all the thoughts I had on Earth that never came to anything. Remembering all those girls I'd ogled and thought I'd like to... but never mind about that. I felt I was going to have a pretty good time of it here. It might have been well worth not having been an axe murderer.

"You wouldn't believe that here in Heaven now," he went on, "there is no use for at least half of the ten commandments. No point in stealing, or hoarding, or fancying. Nobody collects stuff anymore. It drifts, you see! You'd spend all of your time shepherding it like it was a herd of wandering sheep. As for idols, they are ten a penny. Nobody bothers to worship them any more. God's all right; he's one of us... doesn't bother to shave most days."

Just then I was distracted. "Isn't that Marilyn Monroe?" I pointed to a woman walking down the other side of the street.

"Doubtful. Like I said, you can think yourself into being whatever you want. Marilyn is very popular with the women. There are thousands of her."

"I wouldn't mind being like I was sixty years ago," I said.

"Go ahead. Just think it, if you can remember what you looked like. Most of us can't, so we settle for Clarke Gable or Errol Flynn. Yesterday I saw a Rudolf Valentino complete with burnoose and camel. With the influx of the boomers in a few years I'm dreading the number of Elvises we're going to have. The place will be teeming with them."

"Look," I said, "I'm embarrassed to have to ask this, but is sex still a sin?"

"Don't be embarrassed, old chap. Everybody asks that, old or young, male or female. After all, it is the beginning of your new life. If your question is, is there sex in Heaven? the answer is: No and Yes. Sinning doesn't come into it, but there is a problem."

By now I was already halfway into thinking myself into the company of one of the many thousand Marilyn Monroes, possibly as a Clarke Gable, for I certainly didn't want the impediment of a camel. "I don't understand," I said. "I thought you said that all I had to do was think it."

"Yes, yes, that is so, but it's a bit more complicated without matter," and he held his hand out to me and I responded as though to shake hands and our hands passed through each other. "You see," he said, "there is not much point in coveting your neighbour's wife and your neighbour's wife coveting you if all you can do is to walk through each other. Things have been like this for several eternities. There have been a lot of complaints."

I guess he must have seen the disappointed expression on my face, for he went on. "Look," he said, "it's not the end of the world." Then, realizing he had used an unfortunate phrase, he corrected himself. "Things aren't as bad as they seem and... I probably shouldn't be telling you this, but a fellow came up here a few weeks ago... big head of hair... name of Einsteen or Eenstein... something like that... spoke with a German accent. He said that if enough of us were to pack ourselves into the same space there might be an incremental increase in mass which in turn could... ."

The Photographer's Song

"Let me tell you, Dr. Lancit, I was never so relieved as when that woman left. Another martini perhaps?"

"I shouldn't really, Dr. Brandaid—I have a couple of hernia and an arthroscopy this afternoon—but alright, just a small one. It will loosen me up."

"Two more martini, Chelsea, straight up, one with an olive, one with a twist.

"You don't mind, do you—me rattling on like this, but I have just been through the most infuriating two years of my life, and it happened so innocently—the police opening up that derelict house on Castle Hill after suspicious characters were seen hanging around. And there she was, up in the attic, lying peacefully on a divan surrounded by dried flowers. Looked like she had been there for years. Detective Cuff said he thought it might have been some kind of a ritual killing. It gave them all a shock when the coroner found she was still alive. Why they brought her down to my Medical Center instead of The General Hospital, I shall never know. That's when my troubles started.

"It was obvious she was comatose so we put her on life-support and gave her a routine work-up. Nothing showed up. The neurologists came to the conclusion she had perhaps been a flower child and had got into designer drugs. In fact, there was a small puncture in her left index finger. Though no one could explain why she had survived for so long. At first the hospital enjoyed the publicity. It looked as if she would be in for a long stay and we thought we might make a good dollar out of her once we had tracked down her relatives. Besides, she was quite a good looker. I say that professionally speaking of course, Dr Lancit."

"Of course, professionally speaking," said Dr. Lancit, giving Dr. Brandaid a sly wink.

"But soon it dawned on us she was costing a fortune. Three thousand dollars a day just to keep her on life support. We could find no relatives, or next of kin, and she had no insurance. She was driving us into bankruptcy, so after six months or so we gave up on the idea that we could bring her out of the coma and applied to the courts for permission to take her off LS.

"You wouldn't believe what those lawyers charge! And the time they take, months and months. Then we had to fight injunctions by the Right to Life people. Then we had counter injunctions by the Right to Die people. Only the undertakers were on our side. But after several more months we eventually obtained permission to pull the plug. The publicity didn't do us a bit of good, but at least I thought our financial problems were over.

"Another martini, Dr Lancit?"

"Perhaps a small one."

"Two more martini, Chelsea.

"We waited, and we waited, but her condition didn't change. I tell you, Dr. Lancit, after two months off life-support, other than the fact she was unconscious, she was as healthy as you or I. We managed to cut the overhead to $2,500 a day, but then we had trouble with the night nurses. Even for double overtime, they wouldn't work the night shift. They said the cackling scared them. We had the radiators checked. We ripped out the intercom and completely replaced it. We even brought in the Extra Sensory Perception people but although everybody could hear the noises that, I must admit, *did* sound like an old crone cackling, they didn't show up on the tape recordings. We had to get in special security for the night shift and I was back up to $3,000 a day. I tell you, there were times when I would go into that room where she reclined demurely, eyes closed with a beatific smile on her face, and I wanted to clobber her with a baseball bat—professionally speaking of course, Dr. Lancit."

"Of course, Dr. Brandaid. Let me buy this round. Two more martini, Chelsea."

"Then, when word got around, we were bugged by all the medical people. The Mayo Clinic, Johns Hopkins, in fact major hospitals from all over the world sent their experts. Everybody could see the financial benefits if we could just have figured out how to keep other people alive in hospitals without feeding them and in fact without need to pay any attention to them at all. Sometimes I wondered if the poor girl would have enough blood for all the tests they ran, all of which turned up negative.

"Then last Thursday it happened. No doubt you read about it in the newspapers, Dr. Lancit?"

"Most puzzling, Dr. Brandaid."

"We think he was a fancy dress nut boozed up after a night of partying. Barged right into her room, he did, and kissed her full on the mouth. 'That's enough of that, young man!' shouted Nurse Enema, who was on duty at the time, but to her amazement the girl sat up, wide awake and threw her arms around him. Then, picking her up, this clown carried her out to the parking lot, slung her over the pommel of a white horse he had tethered to a parking meter and they galloped off down the main street, Nurse Enema running after them waving the release form and shouting, 'Don't think you can leave without paying the two million, four hundred thousand, three hundred and forty-two dollars and thirty-two cents you owe us!' But they took not a bit of notice.

"The police put out an APB: 'Wanted for abduction: a white male in his mid-twenties wearing a suit of green buckram, thigh-length boots, leather jerkin, Tyrolean hat with feather, and quiver of arrows. The suspect was last seen riding a white horse with a blond, wearing a nightie, slung over his saddle. Anyone with information contact etc., etc.' But they vanished leaving only a trail of horse-potatoes down the main street. As you might guess, I'm praying they never find them.

"Strange though, a number of people came forward to say that on the morning of their disappearance, they kept hearing a woman singing the Photographer's Song."

"The Photographers Song? I don't think I know that one, Dr Brandaid?"

"You must have heard it, Dr. Lancit." Dr. Brandaid cleared his throat and in a fair imitation of a falsetto voice, warbled, "Some day my prints will come..."

"Have another martini, Dr. Brandaid?"

"I think I deserve it, Dr. Lancit."

Love in a Teacup

Ships that Pass

As I stood against the rail
watching the Cunards dash
leaving the navy-riband's trail
I saw another Liner pass.
Out of the variant dark she came,
close on the starboard bow,
a mite too dark to see her name.
Was she The Lorelei?
I saw a figure against the rail
watching the Cunards dash.
In a tumbling sea too loud to hail
I saw her through the glass.
A woman it was I thought I saw.
The wind was in her hair.
A dress of organdy she wore
in the bliss of our brief affair.
I swear I saw her wave her hand
and I waved by return, and
over the waves our loving spanned
till her ghost was left astern.
In the Liner's starry light
we loved with a passion's lure
and passed oblivious in the night
to a memory's sinecure.

1.

He could not forget her face framed in ringlets as he walked down the early morning dark of the bridle path in the quiet desolation of the aftermath of a lost love.

Happiness was quicksilver—the fleeting of all fleeting. Could it be experienced except in retrospect? he wondered.

They had met near the coconut shies. "Hello," he said, over the discordant sounds of the calliope, and she smiled shyly and this gave him the nerve to ask her to join him. She nodded but did not reply, so he took her by the arm and since she did not resist, he walked her towards the shies as though they were a couple. He had no luck. The coconuts were firmly embedded in sawdust but she laughed at his futile attempts. At the shooting gallery he made a winning score. She chose a small teddy bear. As he walked, she held gently onto his arm and he found her presence wonderful.

The daylight was failing now in the yellow-orange glow of the midway lights. The working world fell away into the surrounding darkness. In the clamor of several calliopes, the barkers shouted. Sticky with toffee-apples and candy floss, the crowds jostled. There was sanctity in this fantasy world under the black dome of sky nestled between walls of darkness. Fairy lights had woven the spell of a fairy night, and in the cocoon of sound they were held like stars in a firmament.

On the Ferris Wheel he put his arm around her and she cuddled up to him. They rode the Over-the-Sticks, and the Big Dipper, and she screamed in mock-terror and delight. She was caught unawares on the cakewalk where the need to hang on with both hands left her at the mercy of the blast of air that blew her dress over her head. The farm boys, who had strategically placed themselves for a good look, ogled and jeered. She blushed.

They stood in the crowd in front of the house of horrors listening to the barker boast his attractions—"Roll up! Roll up! See the bearded lady, the Siamese twins, the two-headed snake and the fattest man in the world!" He stood behind her with his arms around her waist, and in the anonymity of the crowds, he thought of slowly raising his hands and fondling her breasts. But he did not. There was vulnerability about her—a delicacy about their relationship as though they were joined by strands of gossamer. He was reluctant to risk the fragile delight of their togetherness. Smiling, she turned her head and looked up at him through a ring of curls. "Are you from Taverton?" he asked, but she turned her head away and did not answer.

In The Tunnel of Love, they kissed with lips that touched like butterflies alighting. Again, he asked where she was from, and again, she would not answer. He wanted to challenge the boxing pro and would have fought for her, but she pulled him away. And as the evening built to its climax, they made their way out of the crowds to the outer limits, to the quiet dark of the fields on one side and the glowing filament of the carnival on the other. They dawdled—he, with his arm about her waist, she, languishing—a gangling of arms and legs almost like a puppet. He talked to her of his father's farm, of tomorrow's plowing. He talked to her of his loneliness. He asked her name. She smiled wistfully but did not answer. Several times he asked her name. Usually she laughed and occasionally, he had the feeling she wanted to tell him. The encroaching quietness of the fields seemed to bring him closer to her. They lay in the sweet grass, her scent mingling with the mown hay. She drew stems of couch across his face until he could no longer bear it, and he kissed her tenderly, marveling at her face ringed in curls. Her dress was high-buttoned about her neck; he thought of unbuttoning it but was afraid she would brush his hand away and the spell would be broken. Then, playfully, she pushed him back, and rising, she ran in short, delicate steps, back into the clamor of the crowds.

He could not bear to be parted from her, afraid he would lose her. She would suddenly appear, here and there, amongst the crowds. She would laugh and wave and lead him on another chase. They were buoyed upon the fairy night. When she wanted to be caught, he caught her, and without regard for people about them, he showered her with gentle kisses. She would desert him and the chase would begin again. Sometimes he was a faun and she was a nymph. Sometimes he was chasing a rainbow. He ached to hold her in his arms. She stirred within him an unexpected tenderness. Losing and finding her by turns was an ecstasy beyond all imagining. Until she disappeared behind a large traction engine that ran the dynamos and he ran around the other way expecting to run into her. But she had disappeared.

He was not concerned. He expected she would surprise him as she had done before, with the touch of her hand upon his sleeve—or her fingers running through his hair. He was drained by disappointment when he could not find her. He revisited the places they had been together, in the vignette of darkness about the fairground's perimeter, the rutted track where they had walked, the flattened grass where they had lain. But there was no sign. He would have called out to her but he did not know her name.

Slowly the crowds dispersed. The canvases on the stalls were tied down. One after another, the rides and the roundabouts closed. The lights, string by string, failed, and as the traction engines stilled, the merriment quieted and the darkness closed. The flaming coal became a lifeless ember. For the first time, he could hear the shuffle of people's feet on the dry dirt. In the sudden quiet, voices sounded remote and far away.

He asked around. Most of the carnies couldn't be bothered to answer. They were too busy packing for tomorrow's move.

"I am looking for a girl."

"So am I mate. Let me know if you find one."

"Have you seen a girl?"

"I've seen a thousand of 'em matey; which one was yours?"

"Her face was ringed in curls," was all he could think to say.

He waited until the last of the lights in the trailer-caravans were extinguished before setting off for the farm. It was a two-hour walk and he had to be up at five for plowing.

He moved sluggishly down the lane. It was an overcast moonless night. He kept close by the hedgerows. Creatures stirred as he disturbed them. At the stile, he cut across the fields in the direction of a train whistle. The only way across the river was by the railway-bridge. He did not cross but made his way down to its abutments on the nearside where the current was stronger. It had been a hot day. The water was comfortably warm, almost like blood. He took off his shirt and left it on the bank. It was a good work-shirt almost new. As he drifted towards the weir a mile downstream he wondered if he should have left his pants. But they were worn, and patched. Not much point in leaving his boots either; who would want one regular boot and one fashioned on a special last for a clubfoot?

2.

In the pin-drop quiet of the night, the girl too, made her way home, sad she would never see him again. She clutched the teddy bear to her. It was kinder this way. Sooner or later he was bound to have found out she could not hear and could not speak.

She should have pulled away when he took her arm, but except for the limp, the boy was good-looking. She had waited all afternoon for Jed Miller. He was to have picked her up in the pony and trap and taken her into Thornton. She guessed his wife might be giving him trouble again. She had gone to the fair later, thinking she might see him there. When the boy came up she went with him, figuring it would be easy to slip away into the crowd if she tired of keeping up the charade or if Jed arrived. She sensed it would not be difficult in the loudness of the fairground, where conversation could only be carried on by shouting, to adopt her shy and silent attitude, which had worked very well with men. Sometimes it was hours before they tumbled to the fact she was dumb; then, it would be over.

She guessed he was a farm boy. His manner was gentle and friendly and she enjoyed the rides, though she had been very fortunate on the Cakewalk when her dress had blown over her head. Thank God she had been uncertain she would run into Jed and had gone home and changed, for he became irate if she wore anything under her dress. She was thankful she had not given the farm boys more than they bargained for. She could ill afford more scandal. As it was, she lived from month to month in a lottery of the unthinkable, for when Jed Miller was into his whiskies and into his women, Jed Miller was without a shred of conscience. She would be dismissed if there were any further suggestion of impropriety. Mr.

Tarrant had made that clear. She needed the work. She was a fine seamstress. In fact, she had sewn Millicent Decker's bridal gown when Millicent had married Jed. But where Jed was concerned, whatever the consequences, she could not help herself.

When the boy asked her name she was tempted to answer. As a young girl, her sister had laboriously, by fingers on cheekbones and lips, taught her to say Sarah, though it came out as Sah-ha, Sah-ha. She was allowed to attend school and learn as best she could, but was so ridiculed by the other children for the noises she made when she tried to speak, that it was not long before she feared to try. She had begun to like the boy and feared that any attempt to sound her name would give the game away.

Sometimes she wished she had not been born with a pretty face and comely figure, so that she would not have to brook the tides of men—the delight of attraction, the agony of repulsion. Every man wanted a pretty girl. No man wanted a dummy.

Vaguely, she remembered the unraveling of her life, the doctor's glum prognosis, and her mother's sadness. Slowly the voices quieted. Silence came gradually until the world kept all of its sounds to itself, and around her people opened and closed their mouths like goldfish and were annoyed when they mistook her remoteness for obstinacy. And soon, it seemed to her there was less difference between waking and sleeping. She could lipread well, and even when they lay together, there was enough light to reveal the boy's hopes and dreams, for they might have been her hopes and dreams too.

There was something more than fun to the game they played. Each time she let him catch her she found it wildly exhilarating, and after each brief tryst of kisses, she found it more difficult to tear herself away. Perhaps this time it would be different. Dare she let him take her home?

It was then she saw Jed. He was coming in on the far side of the fairgrounds with a fancy woman on his arm. She ducked away from the boy and ran around between the traction engines. When she saw the boy was circling in the opposite direction she backtracked, slipped behind the Helter-Skelter and the Haunted House, and was gone. Even with his fancy woman, Jed would have caused trouble. He was a bully of a man. She did not want to see the boy hurt. He would've been no match for Jed even without his game leg. Jed could have given the boxing pro a fist-full.

After she left the fairground, she made her way up a slight rise in a wheat field. Out of sight, amongst the stalks, in the shadows beyond the spill of light, she could watch. The boy was almost frantic now, in search of her. His limp, giving rise and fall to his shoulders, made him easy to track. Bewildered, he wandered without system, scrutinizing the faces around him only to move on when none triggered recognition. Once he passed close and she had to flatten herself in the wheat, fearing he would see her.

She watched Jed and his fancy woman too. She did not know the woman but was not jealous. She knew the score, and was thankful she was not Jed's wife. They went on many of the rides that she and the boy had ridden and now they were standing in the crowd outside the House of Horrors, just as she and the boy had done. She could not see them well, but would have bet that in the intimacy of the crowds, Jed would be holding his fancy woman's buttocks in his hands.

In the silence, she watched the moving panorama slow. One by one the lights extinguished. The boy still searched and asked questions. She was touched.

Jed and his fancy woman had left with the crowds. By now, they would be up in Carley Woods, one of Jed's favorite spots. As usual, he would have left the pony to graze on the common and led his girl into the woods. He was not easily satisfied. This may have been his major attraction to women. A girl was guaranteed at least three courses. But when he was through with his desserts, Jed was not a man to wait on ceremony either. She wondered if his fancy woman of tonight was on her first outing. If so, she was in for a surprise. When Jed finished he would rise, and pulling up his trousers, climb into the trap, whipping the pony into a trot. She knew his habits well, and she could not help but smile at the thought of his fancy woman grabbing shoes, stays, stockings, and whatever she had time to gather, and running after the trap if she were to avoid the four-mile walk back to Lemberton. Apart from the impropriety of "wearing nothing underneath", from the standpoint of Jed's girls, it was a practical necessity. By now she was used to it—used to Jed not bothering to button his fly till they reached the edge of town. You could never be sure when Jed wanted second helpings. Why did she go with this boor of a man?

She watched the moving silence of the pasteboard world before her, the wind rising. She could see the canvas awnings billowing and she tried to remember, from her childhood, the sound of the flap that the billowing canvas made in the wind. The dull clapping sound escaped her; she had forgotten. She tried to imagine the swish of the night breeze as it curled a field of wheat into twisting patterns. She tried to imagine the sound of many people talking. Deafness is not the roar of placing hands over ears. Deafness is a cold, eerie silence that challenges the extremes of nothingness. She knew why she went with Jed Miller. At least he didn't care that she was a dummy. She went with Jed because, when his huge body heaved and sweated above her, he could make her forget her lifetime silence, and for a few seconds, a few minutes, she belonged in his world.

    She watched the fattest man in the world squeeze into the smallest caravan. She watched the bearded lady remove her beard and follow the fattest man in the world into the smallest caravan. She watched the Siamese twins part and go to different lodgings. She waited until the boy limped out through the gate on the far side of the fairgrounds. She was tempted to run after him. She wanted to scream through the purgatory of silence, "Take me with you!"

    She turned towards home. Night was quiet but for the lowing of cattle, and in the distance, a single train's whistle. But she could not know that. The darkness like the deafness took her a further step away from the world. A dry-stone wall ran parallel to the road as she neared the village. Grasping the teddy bear by the feet, she beat its head savagely against the wall until it split and the stuffing flew out. Sobbing, she tried to say Sarah, Sarah and the words came out Sah-ha, Sah-ha. In a rampage of unconstrained breath came nonsensical sounds that she meant to be the words "Damn, damn, damn, damn."

Congratulations on your finding a bottle with a genie.

Genie-in-a-Bottle Inc. hereby notifies you that you are eligible for the customary three wishes.

We are a bona fide company. Our procedures are straightforward and you won't have to kiss a frog or be required to submit to any other unsanitary procedures. We hope that your experience will be both pleasurable and exciting.

<u>Please read the following carefully before wishing:</u>

1) Unless the Company has indicated that your bottle was found during an annual sale, in which case you may be eligible for bonus wishes, your wishes are limited to three. You may not wish for more wishes, for example. Three is your limit.

2) All wishes will count, though wishes will not override wishes. Wishing you had not made the previous wish will not reverse it, but will count as another of your three wishes.

3) Do not wish for example, that the genie go to hell. Wishers will be charged for lost genies.

4) Think before you speak: some wishers have inadvertently made wishes in the course of ordinary

conversation, a complete waste or worse still—a horrible mistake. "Oh God, I wish I could think of an appropriate thing to wish for," might help you with your next wish, but you've wasted one.

5) Think carefully before you wish. On your income can you afford a handsome prince, a beautiful princess who will cater to your every need, your every desire, your every perversion? What will your husband or wife say? Where will the handsome prince/the beautiful princess sleep? Contrarily, where will your wife, your husband sleep? And besides, you've got to feed them. And will they demand at least minimum wage, a car, their own cell phone, holidays with pay? Ask yourself, will a prince or princess used to palatial living in the middle-kingdom be satisfied with a three bedroom ensuite bungalow with a two-car garage? Keep in mind, Federal and Provincial labour laws apply.

6) Also keep in mind we have no return of merchandise policy. All merchandise wished for is "As Is" and comes without warranty. While Princesses and Princes will, in general, meet the description of Beautiful and Handsome, if so wished, the Company cannot guarantee skin condition, freedom from infectious or contagious diseases, personal hygiene, bad breath or pleasantry of disposition.

7) Couch your wishes in the most unmistakable of terms. This can be vitally important, as unclearly stated wishes can result in confusion and unwelcome alternatives to the desires of the wisher. For

example, wishing one would "always have enough money" is vague, and likely to be taken literally as meaning not one penny extra. It is not the same thing as wishing to have, say, $1,000,000 a year for life. We refer you to clause # 6), the "As Is" and no-return policies regarding granted wishes.

8) The offer of three wishes is limited to three minutes from commencement of the first wish.

9) Large articles will be charged delivery

10) Genie-in-a-Bottle Inc. will not be responsible for marriage breakdowns, family disturbances, assault and battery, suicide, homicide or any other catastrophes resulting from the irresponsible choice of wishes.

Congratulations and good luck with your wishes.
  Yours cordially,
  Vice President of Wisheries,
  Genie-In-A-Bottle Incorporated—
  a subsidiary of Meairs, Canada.

Like a Child's Balloon

Strange he should have gone so far back for a memory. It reminded him of when he was a small boy and his mother thumped him on the back after he had swallowed a candy and was in danger of choking. *Thump* it went, and then *thump, thump*, and then *thump* again. Then the thumping stopped and he had the distinct feeling he was floating upwards. He felt a slight bump as he hit the ceiling and drifted into a corner. He felt for all the world as if he were a child's balloon.

Below him, around a bed, he could see a fluster of doctors and nurses in great consternation. A young doctor, holding electrodes, shouted *Clear!* and then there was a *thump, thump* and the bed and the patient jerked in sudden spasm. The young doctor did this several times until an older doctor took him by the arm and Albert Lemster heard him say, "The old fellow is 96, you know." At this, realizing that any success at revival would be short-lived, he laid the electrodes back on the trolley. After a short conversation in medical terms which Albert did not understand, they went out of the room, leaving two nurses to put everything back in order. It was then that he saw the figure on the bed. It came as a shock to find that he was looking down upon himself.

For years, he had not actually seen himself in the mirror as he was. There had been a lag as he had grown older and he had fooled himself that he still looked the way he had looked twenty, thirty, forty years ago. He was shocked when he saw how old he looked, like the mummy they found preserved in ice in the Alps. His skin was thin, bluish parchment stretched tight over his cheekbones. He was relieved when the nurse pulled the sheet up over his face.

Was it even his face? He was not conscious of being part of it any more. But what now? He was not exactly surprised at finding himself in an afterlife. He had lived his life in a loose conglomerate of philosophies, though he had half expected it that it would all be over, and there were a good many people whom he would just as soon not run into again. It was the suddenness. One minute he was eating his supper, the next he was floating around like a ridiculous child's balloon. But since it looked as though he might live forever, he supposed he had better make the best of it. Albert was always a humble person and would never have entertained the idea that God, for all his omnipotence, should greet him. But he did expect a little guidance, from perhaps a lackey, an odd job's person. It would not have surprised him if Heaven were highly organized. A decent set of wrought iron gates, a bit of nicely mowed lawn, perhaps a uniformed commissionaire—"Bangladesh 747 disaster on the right, please, New England Mushroom Gatherers Club far left, sir. Ethnic Cleansing group, center aisle—single file please. Afraid you folks have a long wait."

But was he destined for Heaven? Albert had given considerable thought to the prospect of Hell. Perhaps because he thought it the most likely place for him in the off chance that there was an afterlife. His idea of Hell was to be required to upholster cheap chesterfields for eternity—the kind that were included in complete rooms of furniture for $399. The fabrics would be imitation leopard, tiger or zebra, the predominant colours green and yellow—always green and yellow. On the walls of his workshop he imagined prints of the kind displayed in family restaurants where they warn you that the food is home-cooked. The music of Kenny G would be piped in or Anne Murray singing "Snowbird, Snowbird" forever. It was not a pleasant thought.

He had more difficulty with imagining Heaven. No doubt everything would be soft—the consistency of McDonald's hamburgers. But white, everything would be soft and white, feathers, chiffon, mist and clouds, and for some reason he kept thinking of cream cheese. How Heaven worked was more difficult to fathom. For bliss never seemed to him to be sustainable. His greatest pleasures had always come from contrasts. Drinking hot chocolate with cold hands, a sudden brightening—a shaft of sunlight at the end of a dull monotonous day, the relief from toothache. The prospect of being transported to a state akin to an orgasm for eternity struck him as being worse than upholstering cheap chesterfields, and a good deal more wearing.

But where he was at the moment was neither one place nor the other. You would have thought they would have put up a few signs. But he was stuck, very much like a child's balloon, on the ceiling in the corner of an emergency room in The General Hospital. The prospect of spending eternity here was depressing. Then he discovered he could propel himself. By thinking *left*, he found he could move left. By thinking *right*, he could move right. With more effort he found he could think *down*, for he realized from the beginning that he had a natural force of buoyancy which, when he relaxed, tended to make him rise. He could even, by just thinking about it, move forward.

Tentatively he moved down the wall and towards the door. Tentatively, because he could not shake the feeling that somebody might notice him and if he were questioned it would be difficult to explain. Being invisible took some getting used to. As a nurse left the room he slipped through the door with her. Later he was to find that, with a little more effort, he could pass through doors and walls. The emergency department corridor was typical, all hustle and bustle with people in various stages of anxiety. He would have liked to have gotten out of there, for the place gave him the creeps, but the single window showed that it was dark outside and he, too, felt anxious. It was the feeling he had known many times in cheap motels in strange towns after dark. He thought his way along the corridor until he came to a stairwell. He let himself rise until he was snug under the stairs. It had been a tiring day from what he remembered of it. The tight feeling around his chest, over supper in the Old People's Home. Then he didn't remember any more until the thumping started. He was very tired and he fell into a sound sleep.

It was eight the next morning when he awoke. Light was streaming in through the window. It took him a second or so before he remembered where he was and he mulled over the events of the night before. Could it have been a dream? But if so, where was his body? The thinking method of locomotion still worked, and so he thought himself out from under the stairwell, moved down the corridor, and out through the hospital's main entrance. Moving along to the street corner he found himself in the downtown rush hour. The sidewalk was busy with men and women, carrying cups of coffee and briefcases, making their way to offices. At first he tried to dodge them, fearing he would be bowled over, but then he found, if he relaxed, people could pass through him.

When he reached the junction of Queen and Yonge Streets, a gust of wind caught him and carried him into the path of a streetcar. He was caught up in the spontaneous fear that precedes the inevitability of bodily harm that he had experienced several times during his lifetime, usually when he was at the wheel of a car, and he or somebody else had done some damn fool thing that looked as though it would precipitate an accident. He supposed it was the rush of adrenaline. The streetcar rolled over him. He spun around under the wheel bogies several times before being expelled into the whirling turbulence in its wake. Old habits die hard. He had forgotten he no longer had a body. He was simply a balloon of consciousness over which he had a modest control, for he could still think his way around, though he was finding it more difficult not to rise. He needed considerable concentration to stay low to the ground. Sometimes the effort exhausted him and he sought an overhang or some other projection under which to rest.

Throughout the day he moved about the downtown core. It was a pleasant change to be able to move without a walker, without a wheelchair, without the aches and pains. He couldn't be sure if he was wearing his glasses. He doubted it, yet he could see as well as ever. His mind too seemed sharper. At lunchtime, he sat next to a girl on a bench down by the Flat Iron Building. Even with the effort required to constantly think *downward*, he could have done the crossword in half the time the girl could—just like when he was young. His mind had somehow thrown off the infirmities of his body. He spent the evening in a bar eavesdropping on conversations. A Tiffany lamp hung over each table and he found he could nicely relax under the shade. He was staggered at what people said to each other when they didn't think anyone else was listening. Once, when a martini was left on the bar, he felt the urge to taste the sharp tang of the gin. Though he tried passing through it several times none of its delight rubbed off on him. He pondered that once he had reached his final destination, there might be time from eternally upholstering, or if he went to the other place, the occasional time-out from perpetual ecstasy, when he might snatch an extra dry martini with a twist. The thought buoyed his spirits.

He waited until the bar closed in the early hours before seeking a convenient stairwell under which, once again, he slept.

The day following was Saturday. People in the suburbs mowed lawns, frequented malls. Some had left the previous evening for their cottages. Downtown was quiet. Only those needed to keep the city ticking stayed, along with the homeless and the core of city dwellers in high-rise apartments and swish townhouses. He had the freedom of an invisible voyeur and made the most of it. His amazement at what people did when they thought they were alone, continued. There were very few who were really what they seemed. Only occasionally did he find genuine people who lived life in private as they did in public. The children were the exception; innocent children had no other personalities than the ones that were on show.

Again he spent the evening in a bar. Later he drifted up to the penthouse suite of a premier hotel where he spent the night.

It was a magnificent late-summer Sunday morning that promised a hot dry day. The sky was a blue Heaven. The sun had already warmed the asphalt streets and perhaps it was the rising thermals that gave him even more difficulty in thinking himself *down*. Or perhaps, as an observer, he had seen enough. He began to rise.

Soon the streets and the buildings were beneath him and he was above the Cement Works and the Power Station's stacks. He began to drift west in the gentle breeze. Soon he was clear of the tweed pattern of houses and streets of the town and was drifting over green plaid fields. It was then that he heard the sound of church bells ringing. It took him back to his boyhood—to the days of town clocks, when nobody owned time.

He had never felt an affinity to God except through God's creations. As a boy, on warm summer nights, he would sneak out of the house and climb the escarpment. There, he would lie on his back and watch the stars circling. His favourite time was dawn when the hills were man-quiet. Beneath him now was a quilt of fields, gold squared between corn-green and fallow-brown; one, a single field of ripe wheat larger than the others—like the one in which he had made love to Jenny for the first time. The mind has a habit of assembling memories in what seems like yesterday, as though it cannot be bothered to seek more distant files. How quickly time had passed before they were counting their days together carefully, knowing that fifty years of marriage was a double jeopardy. For, like a big cat, *time* was stalking them and they waited to see which it would forsake at the expense of the other.

After Jenny had gone, it was a matter of waiting. He couldn't climb the hills, anymore and the stars were dim and no longer seemed focused on him. Once he became infirm and couldn't leave the hive of the senior's home, like everyone else, he acquired the habit of listening to the buzz of mankind. But he didn't find God there either.

He was rising now at a faster rate in the cooler air. The fields contracted and soon it was difficult to distinguish one from another for a slight haze. Beneath, several jets passed from east to west *en route* to Vancouver, Los Angeles and Chicago, leaving vapour trails like an unruly child defacing a chalkboard. On the way up he experienced turbulence from wisps of cirrus forming, but now the air was tranquil. He pondered his struggles through life in his passion for success, his attempts to employ his meagre talents to give himself a higher profile, his efforts to stand out above the others. Now he realized success meant only one thing: the satisfaction of looking back upon an exemplary life, and this he could not do. He had done well on sins of commission; he had never set out deliberately to harm anyone. But his record on sins of omission was pathetic: there were so many things he should and could have done, but had not.

Thoughts of eternal upholstering and perpetual ecstasy still drifted through Albert's mind, but now his thoughts seemed to be dispersing into the great communal consciousness. He was having difficulty in determining where he ended and the world began. He felt as if he were expanding, but at the same time there was a tightening about him as though he were wearing a hat that was several sizes too small. Had another soul been there at that moment, it would have heard a loud pop, like the sound of a child's balloon, bursting.

Author photo by Carys Rouleau

Stan White began life in Birmingham, England. He was an industrial photographer before coming to Canada in 1957 where he married and settled in Toronto working as a commercial and advertising photographer. In 1970 he joined Sheridan College as a teaching master and ran the studio for them for 20 years, teaching lighting and product illustration.

After he retired in the early 1990s, he continued with a life-long interest in stereo photography, photographing avidly in and around Brantford. These photographs are now in the local archives. In cooperation with the Photographic Historical Society of Canada, he set up a library of information on stereo photography now housed in the Art Gallery of Ontario.

Throughout his life, he has written non-fiction on various aspects of photography. In his 50s he began to write poetry and short stories. He has been published in local anthologies and has published several books of poetry, some in collaboration with other poets. He also wrote a slim book on tabletop stereo imaging in 1970, *Beyond the Third Dimension*, published in the Netherlands and illustrated with ViewMaster reels.

These days, for relaxation, and in the hopes of slowing down the inevitable aging, he plays the musical saw and the theremin, but keeps the windows closed.

Visit his website: www.stanjwhite.com

www.ingramcontent.com/pod-product-compliance
Lightning Source LLC
Chambersburg PA
CBHW071740150426
43191CB00010B/1643